Life-Study of Hebrews

Messages 53-69

Witness Lee

Living Stream Ministry
Anaheim, CA • www.lsm.org

First Edition, September, 1993.

ISBN 978-0-7363-0964-6
(Complete set, softcover)
ISBN 978-0-87083-672-5
(Messages 53-69, softcover)

Published by

Living Stream Ministry
2431 W. La Palma Ave., Anaheim, CA 92801 U.S.A.
P. O. Box 2121, Anaheim, CA 92814 U.S.A.

Printed in the United States of America

14 15 16 17 18 / 10 9 8 7 6 5

CONTENTS

LIFE-STUDY OF HEBREWS

MESSAGE FIFTY-THREE

A CONTRAST BETWEEN THE SIGHT OF THE OLD COVENANT AND THE SCENE OF THE NEW COVENANT

In this message we come to a very exciting subject—the contrast between the sight of the old covenant and the scene of the new covenant (12:18-24). Paul was undoubtedly marvelous both in the spirit and in the mind. He was a very brilliant man. Like one of today's writers who includes photographs in his books, Paul gave us some pictures in 12:18-24. The two scenes portrayed in these verses not only give us a comparison but also a clear view of the situation of both the old and new covenants.

If we read these seven verses carefully, we can see that there are six items belonging to the old covenant and eight belonging to the new covenant. Six is the number of the old creation, which was made in six days (Gen. 1). Eight is the number of resurrection. The Lord Jesus was resurrected on the first day of the week (John 20:1), which is the eighth day. The six items of the old covenant indicate that the old covenant was on the side of the old creation. The eight items of the new covenant indicate that the new covenant is on the side of resurrection. The number eight signifies a new beginning after the passing of a period of time. A week is the first period of time, and the first day of the second week, the eighth day, is a new beginning. Hence, the number eight signifies resurrection, a new beginning. The new covenant is a new start after the period of the old covenant has passed.

The old covenant was of the law, whose position is that of a concubine. The new covenant is of grace, whose position is that of the proper wife. Sarah, Abraham's wife, symbolizes grace in resurrection, and Hagar, the concubine, symbolizes the law related to the flesh. Paul makes this quite clear in Galatians 4, where he tells us that these two women, Hagar and Sarah, are two covenants, Hagar being the old covenant and Sarah the new. In other words, Hagar stands for the law and Sarah for grace. We Christians today are not the children of Hagar but of Sarah. We are children of grace. These two women also symbolize two mountains. Hagar signifies Mount Sinai, and Sarah signifies Mount Zion, which is the heavenly Jerusalem, our mother.

I. THE SIGHT OF THE OLD COVENANT ON THE SIDE OF THE LAW

A. Comprising Six Items

Let us now look into the six items of the old covenant presented in verses 18 through 21. This side is the side of the law.

1. The Mountain Being Touchable and Set on Fire

Verse 18 says, "You have not come to the mountain which might be touched and which was set on fire." The first item in the sight of the old covenant was the mountain which was set on fire (Exo. 19:11-12, 18). Do you like such a mountain? I prefer a mountain covered with trees and flowing streams, but I do not like a mountain that is set on fire. That would terrify me. Paul seemed to be saying, "Hebrew brothers, do you still want to go back to the old covenant? Don't you know that that belongs to the mountain which was set on fire?" After saying so many things in the foregoing chapters, he showed them such a picture.

2. Darkness

The second item in the sight of the old covenant is darkness (v. 18; Deut. 5:23). Ordinarily, when there is a great fire, there is also some shining and enlightening. But the Bible says that while the fire was burning on Mount Sinai, there was darkness. This darkness came from two sources: from the thick cloud in the air and from the heavy smoke on the earth. The mingling of the cloud and the smoke produced a thick darkness. This picture depicts the negative situation of the old covenant.

3. Gloom

The third item in the sight of the old covenant is gloom (v. 18; Exo. 20:21; Deut. 5:22, Heb.). What is the difference between darkness and gloom? According to my understanding and experience, darkness is objective and gloom is subjective. When darkness is afar off, it remains darkness, but once we enter into it, it becomes gloom. Gloom is an atmosphere in which we dwell. When we enter into darkness and dwell in it, that darkness becomes gloom. Darkness was not only an objective condition for those in the old covenant; it had become the gloom in which they dwelt.

The same is true in our spiritual experience. When we were not seeking the Lord, we were in darkness. But when we began to pursue spiritual things, we immediately had the deep sense that we were in gloom. Before we were revived, we were in darkness. After we were revived, we were in a gloomy situation. If the Hebrew brothers had returned to the old covenant where the darkness was, that darkness would have brought them into gloom.

4. Whirlwind

The next item is the whirlwind (v. 18). A whirlwind is a type of wind that has no direction or peace. In my background in Christianity, there was no direction or peace. Neither was there any direction or peace with the Judaizers. With them there was just the whirlwind.

5. The Sound of a Trumpet

In the sight of the old covenant there is also the sound of a trumpet (v. 19; Exo. 19:13, 16, 19; 20:18). The sound of a trumpet indicates a warning. Religion is filled with warnings, such as, "Don't do this or you will go to hell," or, "Be careful or you will lose your salvation." In religion, they sound the warning trumpet much more often than they deliver a positive message. Religion always says, "Be careful—don't do that," for in religion there are always many more "don'ts" than "do's." The sound of the trumpet is a sign of the poverty of religion. Religion has nothing positive to afford us; it can only warn us negatively. Every religion, including Buddhism, Catholicism, and Protestantism, is the same in principle, sounding warnings and telling us what we should not do.

6. The Terrifying Voice of Words

The sixth item in the sight of the old covenant is the terrifying voice of words (v. 19; Deut. 4:12; Exo. 19:19). What people finally have in religion is the terrifying voice of words, not the jubilant praise to the Lord. However, in the church we always hear the praises to the Lord.

B. All Items Being Temporal

Because all the items in the sight of the old covenant were of the old dispensation they were temporal, not permanent. Just as the old creation will one day pass away, so all the items of the old covenant, belonging to the old creation, have been terminated.

II. THE SCENE OF THE NEW COVENANT ON THE SIDE OF GRACE

A. Comprising Eight Items in Four Pairs

Now we come to the scene of the new covenant on the side of grace (vv. 22-24). This scene comprises eight items in four pairs. That these items are arranged in pairs is very meaningful. The six items of the old covenant are presented singly, while the six items of the word of foundation in Hebrews 6 are arranged in three pairs. Here, in chapter twelve, we have the eight items of the new covenant arranged in four pairs.

1. The First Pair

The first pair consists of Mount Zion (v. 22; Psa. 2:6; Rev. 14:1) and the city of the living God, heavenly Jerusalem (v. 22; 11:10, 16; Rev. 22:2). Here there is no fire but a beautiful mountain with a glorious city, the heavenly Jerusalem, which is God's habitation and the center of His universal administration.

2. The Second Pair

The second pair is composed of the myriads of angels, that is, the universal gathering (v. 22; Rev. 5:11), and the church of the firstborn ones who have been enrolled in the heavens (v. 23; 2:12; Luke 10:20). The Greek word rendered "universal gathering" may also be translated as "festal gathering." This Greek word, *paneguris,* means universal gathering, whole or full assembly, and is used for a gathering of the people to celebrate a public festival, such as the Olympic games. The entire new covenant age is a festival, and the myriads of angels, who are the ministering spirits rendering service to the heirs of salvation (1:14) under the new covenant, are a universal festal gathering celebrating the marvelous festival of "so great a salvation" (2:3), the greatest and most exciting "game" in the universe. The word of the Lord in Luke 15:7 and 10 may indicate this.

As we have seen, the Greek word used by the Apostle Paul for "universal gathering" was used to describe the Olympic games, the greatest and most important public games in ancient Greece. At the time of the Olympic games, the people held a large public gathering. In like manner, huge crowds attend football games in the United States today. The Apostle Paul used the background of the Olympic games to show us that in this universe a game is in progress. The spectators at this game are the myriads of angels who have gathered together to watch it. The game is the race mentioned earlier in this chapter (v. 1). We are qualified to participate in this game, but the angels are not. They are only qualified to be the cheering spectators. In Luke 15:7 and 10, the Lord Jesus said, "There is joy in the presence of the angels of God over one sinner that repenteth." Whenever a sinner is saved, the angels are excited. I wholly believe that the angels in heaven are also very excited about what is happening in the Lord's recovery today. We are playing the greatest game, and the angels are our spectators.

It is very significant that Paul put the myriads of angels together with the church of the firstborn ones who are enrolled in the heavens. We are the firstborn, and they are the spectators; we are the runners, and they are the observers. In a football game, the spectators are always more excited than the players. Although we may not always be excited, the angels are very excited as they observe us. First Peter 1:12, speaking of things which "the angels desire to look into," indicates that the angels are eager to know this gospel game. I do not believe that the cheering angels are very interested in poor Christianity. There is hardly a game there because there is no race there. But there is a real game in the church life today. Whenever we are excited about what is happening in the church life, the angels must be even more excited. The church life has been keeping the angels very excited.

The focus of God's intention in the whole universe is to gain a group of people like us. The angels have been waiting for this for a long time. If there were no games in the United States, many Americans would be waiting, wondering when there would be a game. Likewise, for centuries, the angels, who saw those in Catholicism worshipping idols and burning candles, have been waiting and watching to see a group of real seekers of Jesus. Whenever they see this, they rejoice in a praising way.

3. The Third Pair

As the third pair in the scene of the new covenant, we have God, the Judge of all (v. 23; Gen. 18:25; Psa. 94:2), and the spirits of just men who have been made perfect (v. 23). In this pair, we have the just God as the Judge and the spirits of the just men, who are the Old Testament saints, made perfect through their faith in the types of Christ.

4. The Fourth Pair

The fourth pair is Jesus, the Mediator of the new covenant (v. 24; 8:6; 9:15) and the blood of sprinkling which speaks better than that of Abel (v. 24; 9:12, 14; Gen. 4:10). As we have seen, Jesus is the Mediator of the new covenant. The Greek word, *neos,* here means new, fresh with respect to quality. In this pair, we have not only the Mediator, the Redeemer, of the new covenant, but also the blood of the new covenant.

In this book, the blood of Christ is particularly prominent and crucial. It is the blood of the eternal covenant (13:20), with which the new and better covenant was enacted (10:29). Through this blood, Christ entered once for all into the Holy of Holies and found eternal redemption for us (9:12). By this blood Christ also cleansed the heavens and all things in the heavens (9:22-24). This blood sanctifies us (13:12; 10:29), purifies our conscience to serve the living God (9:14), and speaks better for us than that of Abel (12:24). It is by this blood that we have boldness for entering into the Holy of Holies (10:19). We should not regard this blood common as animal blood. If we do, we shall suffer God's punishment (10:29).

The blood of Christ not only redeems, sanctifies, and purifies; it also speaks. It is the speaking blood, speaking better than the blood of Abel. Abel's blood speaks to God for accusation and vengeance (Gen. 4:10, 15), whereas Christ's blood speaks to God for forgiveness, justification, reconciliation, and redemption. Moreover, this precious blood speaks to God for us saying that by it (as unveiled in this book) the new covenant, which is eternal, has been enacted, and that in this new covenant God must give Himself and all His blessings to the believers in Christ who receive this covenant by faith.

B. All Items Being Eternal

Because the eight items of the new covenant are on the side of resurrection, all of them are eternal, existing forever. Just as the new heaven and new earth will still remain after the old creation has passed away, so these eight items will remain through eternity.

The things mentioned in verses 18 and 19 are earthly or physical, signifying the side of the law, on which side everyone including Moses was terrified (vv. 19-21). The things mentioned in verses 22 through 24 are heavenly or spiritual, in contrast with the earthly and physical things listed in verses 18 and 19, signifying the side of grace. On this side, both the firstborn ones and the spirits of just men are saved by grace. The people under the old covenant came to the side of the law, whereas we Christians under the new covenant come to the side of grace. Hence, we are "not under law but under grace" (Rom. 6:14). This portion of the word, like Galatians 4:21-31, shows us that we are not under the bondage of law but under the freedom of grace to be heirs of inheritance. This is our birthright. We should not give it up by falling away from grace (v. 15), but rather have grace (v. 28). The things on the side of grace are heavenly, but not all are yet in heaven. A great number of the firstborn ones of the church are still on earth, while the spirits of just men, who are the Old Testament saints, are in paradise where Abraham is (Luke 16:22-24, 26) and where the Lord Jesus and the saved thief went after they died on the cross (Luke 23:43).

As we have seen, none of the six items listed on the side of the law is pleasant. Firstly, there is a mountain set on fire! Who would approach such a place! Then, the darkness, the gloom, and the stormy whirlwind. Lastly, the terrifying sound of the trumpet and the solemn warning voice of words. All these together present a fearful sight. On the side of grace, however, everything is pleasant. The eight items here may be considered as four pairs. The elevated Mount Zion and the beautiful heavenly Jerusalem are the first pair, denoting God's habitation and the center of His universal administration. What a lovely place! Then the celebrating jubilant angels, so much related to the heirs of salvation to whom they minister, and the blessed firstborn ones of the church form the second pair in the scene. What a joyful demonstration of an angelic gathering! They celebrate the human heirs of salvation participating in the blessings of the new covenant as the church of the firstborn ones. God, the Judge of all, who is just, and the spirits (their bodies, not resurrected, are not worthy of listing here) of just men, the Old Testament saints, are related together as the third pair, showing how God, being just, justifies the just saints of old because of their faith. Lastly, the dear Lord Jesus, the Mediator of the new covenant, which is "a better covenant," and His precious sprinkled blood, which speaks better things, compose the last pair, indicating that a better covenant has been enacted with His better blood, that He died and has bequeathed this new covenant as a new testament to His believers, and that He is now the Mediator, the Executor, of this new testament to enforce the full realization of all the blessed facts which are contained within it. What a pleasant scene! What a contrast to the sight on the side of the law, where no God, no Savior, and even no angels are mentioned! No wonder not one saved person is seen there! In the scene of grace, there is the justifying God, the Savior who is the Mediator of His new covenant with His speaking blood, the ministering angels with the assembly (the church) of the saved ones, and the spirits of the justified saints. On the side of the law, the sight ends with a terrifying trumpet and the warning words. On the side of grace, the scene ends with a sympathizing Mediator and a vindicating speaking. After looking at such a contrast, who would be so foolish to leave the side of grace and turn to the side of the law? All eight things on the side of grace are not only heavenly or spiritual but also eternal. Hence, even when the heaven will be shaken (v. 26), these eight things, which are eternal, will still remain (v. 27).

LIFE-STUDY OF HEBREWS

MESSAGE FIFTY-FOUR

AN UNSHAKABLE KINGDOM

In this message we come to a very sober matter—the unshakable kingdom (12:25-29). The kingdom which we are receiving is unshakable (v. 28). Since this kingdom is unshakable, it is neither of the earth nor of the heavens. This is a strong word. Because we have such a doctrinal mind, we may argue with this statement, saying, "What about the kingdom of heaven? Doesn't the Bible speak of this?" Yes, the New Testament does speak of the kingdom of the heavens, but it also says that heaven will be shaken (v. 26; Hag. 2:6). That heaven will be shaken proves that the kingdom which we are receiving is not of heaven. Although there seems to be a contradiction between the terms unshakable kingdom and the kingdom of the heavens, later on we shall see that there is actually no contradiction here.

I. FOR THE OLD COVENANT, THE EARTH BEING SHAKEN AS A WARNING UPON EARTH

For the old covenant, the earth was shaken as a warning upon earth (vv. 25-26; Exo. 19:18). When the old covenant was given at Mount Sinai, the earth was shaken. That shaking was a warning to the people on earth.

II. FOR THE NEW COVENANT, NOT ONLY THE EARTH BUT ALSO THE HEAVEN TO BE SHAKEN AS A WARNING FROM HEAVEN

One day, for the new covenant, not only the earth but also the heaven will be shaken as a warning from heaven. This is according to the word in Haggai 2:6.

III. ONLY THE LORD AND THE THINGS COMING OUT OF HIM REMAINING FOREVER

The earth and the heavens are shakable. Only the Lord and the things that come out of Him will remain forever (v. 27; 1:11; 13:8). This means that the kingdom which we are receiving has come out of the Lord Himself. Hebrews 1:11, speaking of the heavens and the earth says, "They shall perish, but You remain; and they all shall become old as a garment."

The kingdom is actually the Lord Himself as the kingship within us. We have seen that faith is the Lord Himself as the believing element within us. Now, in the same principle, the kingdom is the Lord Himself as the kingship. As a help in realizing this matter, let us read Daniel 2:34 and 35. "Thou sawest till that a stone was cut out without hands, which smote the image upon his feet that were of iron and clay, and brake them to pieces. Then was the iron, the clay, the brass, the silver, and the gold, broken to pieces together, and became like the chaff of the summer threshingfloors; and the wind carried them away, that no place was found for them: and the stone that smote the image became a great mountain, and filled the whole earth." The stone cut without hands is the heavenly Christ who was cut on the cross without human hands. Verse 44, referring to the toes of the image, says, "In the days of these kings shall the God of heaven set up a kingdom, which shall never be destroyed: and the kingdom shall not be left to other people, but it shall break in pieces and consume all these kingdoms, and it shall stand forever." Verse 45 also speaks of the stone, saying, "The stone was cut out of the mountain without hands" and "it brake in pieces the iron, the brass, the clay, the silver, and the gold." These verses indicate that the stone, which is Christ, will eventually become a great mountain filling the whole earth. This great mountain is the coming kingdom. Hence, the unshakable kingdom which we are receiving is Christ with His enlargement.

IV. THE KINGDOM, COMING OUT OF THE LORD, BEING UNSHAKABLE

A. We Having Repented for the Kingdom

The gospel which the New Testament has preached to us is the gospel of the kingdom (Matt. 3:1-2; 4:17, 23; 10:7; 24:14). We repented for the kingdom (Matt. 3:2). Perhaps when we were saved, we did not hear such a clear gospel. At that time, we were afraid of going to hell and desired to go to heaven. Thus, we repented for heaven. This is the preaching of the wrong gospel, for repentance is not for heaven but for the kingdom.

B. We Having Been Reborn into the Kingdom

We have been reborn, regenerated, into the kingdom. In John 3:5 the Lord Jesus said, "Truly, truly, I say to you, unless a man is born of water and the Spirit, he cannot enter into the kingdom of God" (Recovery Version). Many of us were wrongly told that regeneration is for going to heaven. Here we see clearly that regeneration is for entering into the kingdom of God.

C. We Having Been Translated into the Kingdom

Colossians 1:13 says, "Who hath delivered us from the authority of darkness, and hath translated us into the kingdom of the son of his love" (Gk.). This verse reveals that we have been translated out of one kingdom, Satan's kingdom of darkness, into another kingdom, the kingdom of the Son of God's love.

D. The Church Life Being the Kingdom of God Today

In the church, we are living in the kingdom of God today. Romans 14:17 is a strong proof that today's church life is the kingdom: "The kingdom of God is not eating and drinking, but righteousness and peace and joy in the Holy Spirit" (Recovery Version). Revelation 1:9 also proves that we are in the kingdom of God today: "I John, who also am your brother, and companion in tribulation, and in the kingdom and patience of Jesus Christ." When John wrote the book of Revelation, he was already in the kingdom of God. These two verses are a strong proof that the church today is the kingdom. However, as we shall see, what we are in now in the church today is the kingdom in its reality, whereas the kingdom in its manifestation will come with Christ's return in the future.

V. THE REALITY AND MANIFESTATION OF THE KINGDOM

If we would understand the New Testament truths regarding the kingdom, we must realize the two main aspects of the kingdom—the aspect of its reality and the aspect of its manifestation. In the church today, we do not have the kingdom in manifestation; we have the kingdom in reality. According to the outward appearance, men cannot see the kingdom in the church. Nevertheless, the kingdom is a reality among us.

A. The Reality of the Kingdom Being an Exercise and Discipline in the Church Today

The reality of the kingdom, the kingdom in its reality, is an exercise and discipline for us in the church today (Matt. 5:3, 10, 20; 7:21). Suppose you purchase a hamburger at a stand and the cashier gives you too much change. If you are exercised and are ruled by the kingdom, you will return this extra change immediately. This is an experience of the rule of the reality of the kingdom, which is both an exercise and a discipline.

The situation of today's Christianity is very poor, for many Christians have been drugged, thinking that everything is of grace and that there is no need for training, exercise, or discipline. But we realize that we must uplift the standard of the church life through the discipline and exercise of the reality of the kingdom. Through the years, I have seen the Lord's grace working in so many of us. I thank the Lord that there has been a great improvement in His recovery. Nevertheless, we must uplift the standard even higher. If we do this, our cheering angels will be very happy, for they will see a group of believers who are quite serious regarding God's eternal purpose. How we need the discipline for the kingdom today!

B. The Manifestation of the Kingdom Being a Reward and an Enjoyment in the Millennial Kingdom in the Coming Age

The manifestation of the kingdom, the kingdom in its manifestation, will be a reward and an enjoyment to us in the millennial kingdom in the coming age (Matt. 16:27; 25:21, 23). Today, in the reality of the kingdom, we have the exercise and the discipline. In the coming age, in the manifestation of the kingdom, we shall have a reward and an enjoyment. If we read Matthew 16:27 in its context, we shall see that the Lord's coming to reward every man according to his work is related to the manifestation of the kingdom. In Matthew 25:21 and 23, the Lord says to His faithful servants, "Well done, thou good and faithful servant: thou hast been faithful over a few things, I will make thee ruler over many things: enter thou into the joy of thy lord." To enter into the joy of the Lord is to be in the manifestation of the kingdom during the thousand years.

C. Taking the Spirit's Exercise and God's Discipline Today and Receiving the Lord's Reward and Entering into the Sabbath Rest in the Coming Age

If we take the Spirit's exercise and God's discipline in the reality of the kingdom today, we shall receive the Lord's reward and enter into the enjoyment of the coming Sabbath rest (4:9) in the manifestation of the kingdom in the coming age. If we do not accept the Spirit's exercise and God's discipline today, we shall miss the coming kingdom in its manifestation as a reward. We shall not be rewarded with the manifestation of the kingdom at the Lord's coming back; we shall have no right to enter into the glory of the kingdom to participate in Christ's reign in the millennial kingdom; and we shall lose our birthright to inherit the earth in the coming age, to be the royal priests serving God and Christ in His manifested glory, and to be the co-kings with Christ ruling over all the nations with His divine authority (Rev. 20:4, 6).

D. Missing the Coming Kingdom and Losing Our Birthright in the Coming Age Meaning That We Shall Lose the Reward

To miss the coming kingdom and to lose our birthright in the coming age does not mean that we shall perish, but that we shall lose the reward. Although we may lose the reward, we shall never lose our salvation (1 Cor. 3:14-15). Our salvation is secured forever. But whether or not we receive the reward and the birthright in the manifestation of the kingdom depends upon our exercise today.

E. The Warnings in Hebrews Referring to the Suffering of the Loss of the Kingdom Reward and to Being Punished by God

As we have seen, the loss of the reward in the coming kingdom, the forfeiture of our birthright, does not mean that we shall perish. It means that we shall lose the reward and suffer loss, but still "be saved, yet so as through fire" (1 Cor. 3:14-15, Gk.). This is the basic concept upon which all the five warnings of this book are given and with which they all are pervaded (2:3; 4:1-11; 6:8; 10:27, 29-31; 12:25). All the negative points of these warnings are related to suffering the loss of the reward in the coming kingdom and to being punished by God, whereas all the positive points are related to the reward and enjoyment of the kingdom. All the seven epistles in Revelation 2 and 3 are concluded with the same concept—the reward of the kingdom or the loss of it. Only with this concept can the word in Matthew 5:20;

7:21-23; 16:24-27; 19:23-30; 24:46-51; 25:11-13, 21, 23, 26-30; Luke 12:42-48; 19:17, 19, 22-27; Romans 14:10, 12; 1 Corinthians 3:8, 13-15; 4:5; 9:24-27; 2 Corinthians 5:10; 2 Timothy 4:7-8; Hebrews 2:3; 4:1, 9, 11; 6:4-8; 10:26-31, 35-39; 12:16-17, 28-29; Revelation 2:7, 10-11, 17, 26-27; 3:4-5, 11-12, 20; and 22:12 be rightly understood and properly applied. Apart from this concept, the interpretation of these verses will fall either into the extreme objectiveness of the Calvinist school, or the extreme subjectiveness of the Arminian school. Neither of these schools has seen the reward of the kingdom, and even the more they have not seen the suffering of the loss of the kingdom reward. Hence, both consider all the negative points in these verses as perdition. The Calvinist school, believing in eternal salvation (that is, once a person is saved, he shall never perish), refers all these negative points to the perdition of false believers; while the Arminian school, believing that a saved person shall perish if he falls, applies them to the perdition of fallen saved persons. But the complete revelation of the Bible refers these negative points to the suffering of the loss of the kingdom reward. Salvation is eternal: once we get it, we shall never lose it (John 10:28-29). But we may suffer the loss of the kingdom reward, even though we still shall be saved (1 Cor. 3:8, 14-15). All the warnings in Hebrews do not refer to the loss of eternal salvation, but to the loss of the kingdom reward. The Hebrew believers had received the kingdom, but they would have lost the reward in the manifestation of the kingdom if they shrank back from the grace of God, from God's new covenant way. This was the main concern of the writer's warning regarding the staggering Hebrew believers.

Some Christian teachers say that the slothful servant in Matthew 25 is a false servant. But this is altogether illogical. Although one of your children may be slothful, this does not mean that he is false. Since some Christian teachers do not see the matter of the kingdom reward, they must say that the slothful servant is a false servant. On the contrary, some say that the slothful servant is a real servant who has fallen away and lost his salvation.

We have seen that God's original intention was to have a corporate man to express Him with His image, to represent Him with His dominion, and to take possession of the earth. This is the proper human living. Because man fell from God's original intention, God came in to redeem and save us. This is God's salvation, in which there is the birthright having three aspects: being the priests to express God with His image, being the kings to represent God with His dominion, and taking full possession of the lost earth for God's eternal purpose. If we live in this birthright, we shall spontaneously be in the reality of the kingdom of God, for the reality of the kingdom of God is the living out of the birthright, the realization of the full birthright. Since not all Christians are willing to cooperate with God in this matter, He, in His wisdom, has decided to make the birthright a reward. If we take grace, enter into the Holy of Holies, and cooperate with God, we shall certainly live out the birthright. Then whatever we live out will be the reality of the kingdom today. The reality which we are living out today will become our reward in the manifestation of the kingdom. This is the fulfillment of God's original intention. It is also our perfection, glorification, and the gaining of our soul in the coming age. As a result, we shall have the proper human living with an uplifted and resurrected humanity. This is the crucial focus of the entire Bible, and the Bible is very consistent about it. How can all this be worked out? Only by our turning to the spirit, entering into the Holy of Holies, experiencing Christ in all His riches, and allowing the law of life to take us from one stage of glory to another as it permeates us, saturates us, and conforms us to His image.

Hebrews 12:29 says, "Our God is also a consuming fire." God is holy. Holiness is His nature. Whatever does not correspond with His holy nature, He, as the consuming fire, will consume. If the Hebrew believers had turned aside to Judaism, which was common (unholy) in the sight of God, it would have made them unholy, and the holy God, as the consuming fire, would have consumed them. God is not only righteous but also holy. To satisfy God's righteousness we need to be justified through the redemption of Christ. To meet the demands of His holiness we need to be sanctified, to be made holy, by the heavenly, present, and living Christ. Romans stresses the matter of justification (Rom. 3:24) for God's righteousness (Rom. 3:25-26), whereas Hebrews emphasizes the matter of sanctification (2:11; 10:10, 14, 29; 13:12) for God's holiness (12:14). For this, the Hebrew believers had to separate themselves from unholy Judaism unto the holy God who has fully expressed Himself in the Son under the new covenant; otherwise, they would have defiled themselves with their old, profane religion and suffered the holy God as the consuming fire. That would have been "fearful" (10:31)! No wonder Paul was very much concerned about "the terror [fear] of the Lord" (2 Cor. 5:11).

The focal point of the book of Hebrews is to bring us into the holy nature of God. If we do not cooperate with God in this, we shall break His administration. To break God's administration is a governmental matter. Breaking God's law is not as serious as breaking His government. God has revealed that if we do not cooperate with Him in His administrative economy but rather break His government, He will punish us. This means that we shall lose the kingdom reward on the positive side and suffer punishment on the negative side. In Hebrews 10 and 12 we see the way, the race, and the pathway that we must take, run on, and pass through. In these chapters we also see the punishment, the reward, and the kingdom. These three things are crucial aspects of the basic concept in the composition of this book.

No other book in the New Testament reveals the focal point of God's economy as clearly as the book of Hebrews does, for no other book points us to the Holy of Holies and to the law of life in the ark. Although Romans 8:2 does mention the law of the Spirit of life, Hebrews covers the law of life much more thoroughly than Romans does. The writer of Hebrews warns us to take the revelation of God's economy as found in this book. If we take it, we shall receive a reward in the manifestation of the kingdom. If we do not take it, we shall suffer some punishment due to our breaking of God's administrative economy. Those who do not have the substantiating sense, or who fail to exercise it, cannot see this. While we are so serious and sober about this matter, many other Christians are not. Under the enlightening of the heavenly revelation we have been seeing in these messages, we must be serious and sober about running the race on the straight paths. The way we run today will determine our future destiny.

Although we are concerned about our future destiny, we must have the grace to say to the Lord, "Lord, by Your grace I do not care for my destiny—I care for Your economy. You take care of my destiny, and I'll take care of Your economy. Lord, I want to cooperate with You, not for the sake of my future destiny, but for the sake of Your economy today. I want to see that Your economy, which has not been carried out through the centuries, will be fulfilled in these days." We all need to have such a clear vision and be brought on so that God's purpose might be fulfilled among us. God wants to bring a group of His sincere seekers into the Holy of Holies that they might experience the working of the law of life and thus become the corporate reproduction of the standard model, His Firstborn Son. The Lord's coming back depends upon this corporate reproduction. It is impossible for the Lord to come back until this has been accomplished. His having the reproduction of the standard model depends upon the working of the law of life within us. As we have seen, the law of life is neither in the outer court nor in the Holy Place; it is in the ark of testimony in the Holy of Holies. Therefore, we must enter into the Holy of Holies, plunge into the ark of testimony, and experience the law of life. We know where the law of life is—it is in our spirit. Now we just need to say, "Lord, by Your mercy and grace, I am here to cooperate with You. I am ready for You to go on. Lord, do everything You can and whatever You like. I don't care for my future destiny. I only care for Your recovery in today's economy, for the proper recovery of the church life. Lord, may all Your seekers be brought into this way for the fulfillment of Your will!" This is the Lord's recovery in His economy today.

LIFE-STUDY OF HEBREWS

MESSAGE FIFTY-FIVE

TEN PRACTICAL VIRTUES FOR THE CHURCH LIFE

Apparently, the book of Hebrews does not touch the matter of the church. Actually, it is absolutely for the church, because the church is the consummation of God's economy. In Hebrews 2 we clearly see that the resurrected Christ with His uplifted humanity is for the church. According to 2:12, after His resurrection Christ came back to His brothers and, in the midst of the church, He sang hymns of praise unto the Father. In this verse the church is clearly and definitely mentioned in a very deep way. By this we see that Hebrews is not only a book on Christ; it is a book on Christ for the church.

Hebrews 10:25 says not to forsake the assembling of ourselves together. As we have pointed out, for the Hebrew believers to forsake the assembling of themselves together with the saints meant that they were forsaking the new covenant way. When the believers assembled themselves together in ancient times, that assembly was the practical and actual church.

As we have seen, in 12:18-24, we have a contrast between the sight of the old covenant and the scene of the new covenant. In the scene of the new covenant, we see Mount Zion, God's holy city, the myriads of celebrating angels, and the church of the firstborn ones. The church is the center of this scene. After the mention of the church, we have the justifying God, the justified spirits of the ancient saints, and Jesus, the Mediator of the better covenant with His precious blood that speaks better than that of Abel. By this we can see that the church is the focus of the scenery of the new covenant.

In this message we come to chapter thirteen. Although

the word church is not found in this chapter, the entire chapter is concerned with the church life. The experiences of Christ (vv. 8-15) and the ten practical virtues (vv. 1-7, 16-19) covered here are for the church. Nearly everything mentioned in verses 1 through 7 and 16 through 19, such as brotherly love and hospitality, is for the church life, not just for the Christian life. If we would have the proper church life, we need all ten of these virtues. Let us now consider each of them.

I. BROTHERLY LOVE

Verse 1 says, "Let brotherly love continue." No one can say that brotherly love is not for the church life. If we were not in the church life, we would not need brotherly love, for we would be far away from one another and would not need to love one another. But because we have been flocked together, we need brotherly love to continue.

Every local church passes through a honeymoon period. I believe that all the churches in the United States and Canada have passed through their honeymoon. After the honeymoon is over, every newly married couple will eventually have a collision. In order to stay married, we must have the marriage love. In the church we need brotherly love, and in our families we need marriage love.

First Corinthians 13:13 says, "And now abideth faith, hope, love, these three; but the greatest of these is love" (Gk.). According to this verse, love is the greatest virtue. It is also the most excellent way (1 Cor. 12:31, Gk.). The most excellent way is not the way of gifts or teachings but the way of love. Love is the most excellent way because it is the expression of life (1 Cor. 13:1). Love is just life appearing in another form. In 1 Corinthians 8:1, Paul says, "Knowledge puffeth up, but love buildeth up" (Gk.). If we would be built together, we must have brotherly love.

II. HOSPITALITY

Verse 2 says, "Do not be forgetful of hospitality, for through this some have entertained angels without knowing it." How we need hospitality in the church life in the Lord's recovery today. No one can estimate how much hospitality has built up the Lord's testimony since the beginning of the Lord's recovery in this country. Hospitality truly edifies. It brings much new blood into the fellowship of the Body. How we thank the Lord for this! In Romans 12:13 we are told to pursue hospitality, and in 1 Timothy 3:2, Titus 1:8, and 1 Peter 4:9 (Gk.) we are admonished to be hospitable. Among us, brotherly love should continue and hospitality should not be forgotten.

III. REMEMBERING THE SUFFERING MEMBERS

Verse 3 says, "Remember the prisoners as bound with them, and those who are ill-treated as being yourselves also in the body." Remembering the suffering members is undoubtedly for the church life. If we remember the suffering members, it means that we are living in the Body and have the sense of the Body. When one member suffers, all the members sense it and suffer with him (1 Cor. 12:26). This is the Body life. Hence, to remember the suffering ones is a function in the Body, in the church life.

IV. HOLDING MARRIAGE IN HONOR

Verse 4 says, "Let marriage be held in honor among all, and the bed undefiled; for fornicators and adulterers God will judge." Apparently this is unrelated to the church life. However, marriage is a very important factor in the church life. Whether a church is sound and healthy or loses its element and essence is very much dependent upon the marriage life. Do not consider the matter of marriage to be a light thing. We must hold it in honor. This means that we must possess our body, our vessel, in sanctification and honor (1 Thes. 4:3-4), that "no man go beyond and defraud his brother in any matter" (1 Thes. 4:6). In the church life, the brothers and sisters must contact one another in a holy way. This means that we honor our marriage and others' marriage. To honor marriage means to possess our body in sanctification and honor and to flee fornication.

In the church life, contacts between the brothers and sisters are unavoidable. Hence, for our protection from falling into defilement, we must hold marriage in honor and not behave loosely. This is a matter which seriously affects our birthright in God's economy. Reuben lost it due to his defilement (Gen. 49:3-4; 1 Chron. 5:1), and Joseph received it because of his purity (1 Chron. 5:1; Gen. 39:7-12). God will judge fornicators and adulterers, and the church also must judge them (1 Cor. 5:1-2, 11-13). Nothing damages the saints and the church life so much as this defilement.

Verse 4 says that God will judge the fornicators and adulterers. Hebrews is a book concerning God's holiness. The holy God will never tolerate any defilement among us. He will judge His people (10:30; 12:23).

V. WITHOUT LOVE OF MONEY

Verse 5 says, "Let your way of life be without love of money, being satisfied with your circumstances." Surely money-lovers cannot enter into the reality of the church life. Every money-lover is a Judas, a traitor, betraying the Lord, the Lord's testimony, and the church life. It is impossible for such a person to live the church life.

Verse 5 also tells us to be satisfied with our circumstances, for the Lord has said, "I will by no means cease to uphold you, neither by any means will I forsake you." We must be satisfied with whatever we have and with whatever circumstances we are in, knowing that we have the Lord and that we can trust in Him for our living. We should always be satisfied with our circumstances that we may not be distracted from the church life by mammon. Since we have the Lord as our helper, we should be content and at peace that we may be fully kept in the enjoyment of the church life.

By the Lord's mercy and grace, I, an old man, can give a strong word of testimony to the young people. I can assure you that you have no need to worry about your living. Our God is our Father, and He knows all we need. I can still remember the day when the Lord forced me to give up my job for His ministry. I had been struggling with the Lord about this for approximately three weeks. On that last day, August 23, 1933, I went to the Lord at midnight. Before that time, I had received from Him the word in Matthew 6:33, which says that if we seek God's kingdom and righteousness, the Lord will add to us whatever we need for our daily living. That night I went to the Lord to make a thorough deal with Him about whether it was His will that I leave my job for the sake of full-time ministry. But when I went to Him, He did not give me time to pray. He just rebuked me, telling me that He had already given me a word from Matthew 6. The Lord said, "If you believe it, take it. If you don't believe it, that's all." Suddenly I had the feeling that the Lord had left me and that His presence was gone. I was unable to pray any further. I could not even say, "In the name of the Lord Jesus, Amen." As I was kneeling there, I wept and said, "Okay, Lord, I take Your word." From that day until now, I have never lacked anything. The Lord knows our need. We may have the peace to sacrifice everything for the Lord and for the church life, not worrying about our living. As long as we enter within the veil and go outside the camp, the Lord will take care of our needs. He is our Helper and He never forsakes us. Our responsibility is to live in the Holy of Holies. Our life is in Him, and our living is in His hands. Praise Him that He is so living and real!

VI. REMEMBERING THE MINISTERS OF THE WORD OF GOD

Verse 7 says, "Remember the ones leading you, who have spoken to you the word of God, and considering the issue of their manner of life, imitate their faith." This is essential in the church life. Verse 7 is a continuation of verses 5 and 6. Their "manner of life" here must refer to the way of life pursued by those ministers of the word of God—without love of money and being satisfied with their circumstances. Their "faith" must refer to the fact that they trusted in the Lord, who is their Helper, for their living. The word which they ministered and the life which they lived should all be Christ, and their faith should be the faith in Christ, of which Christ is both the Author and Perfecter (12:2). Such a manner of life and such a faith are surely worthy of imitation by the believers.

The ministers of the word of God should have a manner of life that issues in an example of faith for the church members, the receivers of the word of God, to imitate. Then the church members will not only receive the word they minister, but also imitate their faith expressed in their manner of life. Their manner of life should be that of trusting in the Lord for all their needs. How different this is from the worldly manner of life! As the believers consider the issue of the manner of life of those who minister the word of God to them, they will be influenced to imitate their faith in God.

VII. DOING GOOD

Verse 16 says, "Do not be forgetful doing good and sharing with others, for with such sacrifices God is well pleased." This verse speaks of doing good. This is not the good of good and evil; it is the good in God's economy. Doing good according to God's economy, which is a sacrifice well-pleasing to God, is according to God's working within us (Eph. 2:10; Phil. 2:13), that is, according to the working of the law of life. Our outward doing good must be according to the inward working of the law of life.

VIII. SHARING WITH OTHERS

Verse 16 also speaks of sharing with others. This is necessary for a proper church life. It is really improper if in the church some needy saints are not well cared for. This means that the sharing with others is absent or inadequate. Sharing with others is also a sacrifice well-pleasing to God. Its purpose is to supply the want of the needy saints for equality (2 Cor. 8:14-15). Those who have more than they need should share with those who have less than they need. When those who have more share with those who have less, there will be an equality among us. This is similar to the gathering of manna by the children of Israel in the wilderness. In those days, "He that had gathered much had nothing over; and he that had gathered little had no lack" (2 Cor. 8:15; Exo. 16:18). As a result, there was equality among the children of Israel.

IX. OBEYING THE LEADING ONES AND SUBMITTING TO THEM

Verse 17 says, "Obey the ones leading you and submit to them, for they watch over your souls as those who will give account, that they may do this with joy and not groaning, for this would be unprofitable to you." I have heard of many so-called spiritual people who say that as long as we have the Spirit, we all are leading ones and we do not need anyone to lead us. They say that it is wrong to have leaders among us. According to them, having leading ones means to have an organization with a hierarchy and a pope. We must be balanced in this matter. We thank the Lord that in His recovery during the past fifty years there have always been the proper leading ones among the churches for the keeping of the order in God's house.

In every household there are, in addition to the parents, the older brothers and sisters. Suppose there are six children in a family. Spontaneously, each one of them knows his order. When the oldest brother speaks, all the others listen to him. But if the third brother would presume to be the oldest brother, all the others would refuse to listen to him. If we would maintain a good order in the house of God, we must have the leading ones, and all the saints must obey them and submit to them. This is necessary for the building up of the church.

This matter of leadership, however, should not be too official. For example, in a family there is no need for the oldest child to say, "I am the number one child, and you all must realize that I am the leader of the children in this family. Since I have this position, I am God's deputy authority." I am sorry that the leaders of many Christian groups have utilized the book, *Spiritual Authority,* written by Brother Nee. They have used this book to build up their empire, saying, "I am the spiritual authority here. According to Watchman

Nee's book, you all must listen to me." Some time ago, three young men came from a certain place to visit the elders of the church in Anaheim. They rebuked the elders, saying, "Are you elders? You don't know how to be elders. We are elders." These young men, all of whom were in their early twenties, were just boy elders, having been established by some self-appointed king. They were not true elders; they were actors.

If a brother is truly an elder, everyone will realize it, and he will have no need to assume any authority. If you are the oldest child in a family, all the other children realize this. There is no need to exercise yourself to assume authority. Rather, you should take loving care of your younger brothers and sisters. Likewise, the elders in the churches should not assume authority but take loving care of the saints. Elders, forget your authority. On their side, the saints must obey you and submit themselves to you. On your side, however, you should not assume authority. Nothing is uglier than assuming authority. We should simply be what we are without assuming anything. Nevertheless, in the house of God and for the building up of the Body of Christ, we must have a beautiful order among us.

X. PRAYING FOR THE APOSTLES

Verses 18 and 19 say, "Pray for us, for we are persuaded that we have a good conscience, desiring in all things to conduct ourselves rightly. And I beseech you much more to do this that I may be restored to you more quickly." Praying for the apostles is also an aspect of the church life. To pray for the apostles is not to pray in a personal and private way; it is to pray for the ministry and to participate in the Lord's move for the fulfilling of God's purpose. I thank God for the prayer meetings in Anaheim. Every week we spend a long time praying for the Lord's move on earth and for the fulfilling of His purpose.

As we consider these ten virtues, we see that they are all necessary for the church life and should be practiced among us.

LIFE-STUDY OF HEBREWS

MESSAGE FIFTY-SIX

THE EXPERIENCES OF CHRIST FOR THE CHURCH LIFE

In this message we come to the experiences of Christ for the church life (13:8-15). Before I come to this matter, however, I am burdened to say a further word about the way, the race, and the paths, particularly about the one race becoming the many paths.

By looking at the arrangement of the furniture in the tabernacle, we can see how Christ is the way and the race, and how the one race becomes many paths. As we have seen, the altar and the laver are in the outer court; the showbread table, the lampstand, and the incense altar are in the Holy Place; and the ark, containing the golden pot, the budding rod, and the table of the testimony, is in the Holy of Holies. The altar, laver, incense altar, and ark form a line, and the showbread table and the lampstand form an intersecting line. These two lines form a cross. Each of these items signifies an aspect of Christ.

Consider the experience of a sinner who comes to Christ. Firstly, he comes to the altar where he kneels down, makes confession, and takes Christ as his substitute, Redeemer, and Savior. Here at the altar he begins to enjoy Christ. After experiencing Christ at the altar, he goes to the laver, which signifies that the Redeemer has become the life-giving Spirit (1 Cor. 15:45b; 2 Cor. 3:17), and there he experiences the washing of the living water. The washing of the water in the laver is different from the washing of the blood at the altar. The blood at the altar washes away our sins; the water of the laver washes away the earthly dirt.

While many Christians go back and forth between the altar and the laver, the laver and the altar, we need to take a straight path into the Holy Place. Once we are in the Holy Place, we make a right turn to the showbread table where we enjoy Christ as the bread of life. Before coming into the church, we never heard that Christ was eatable. But the Lord Jesus said, "I am the bread of life," and "He who eats Me shall also live because of Me" (John 6:48, 57, Recovery Version). Now, after coming into the church, we have been helped to eat Christ, to feed on Him, and even to masticate Him. After feeding on Christ at the showbread table, we must make an about-face and take a straight path to the lampstand. Here at the lampstand we are enlightened by the light of life (John 1:4), that is, by the light which comes from feeding on Christ. At the lampstand we make another about-face to the central line, and then make a left turn and go to the incense altar to experience Christ in resurrection as the sweet fragrance by which we are accepted of God. This experience of the incense altar will then usher us directly into the Holy of Holies. In the tabernacle we can see several paths: the path from the cross to the laver, from the laver to the showbread table, from the showbread table to the lampstand, from the lampstand to the incense altar, and from the incense altar to the ark in the Holy of Holies. Once we are in the Holy of Holies, we are in the shekinah glory. But we should not stop there. We must proceed even further and experience all the contents of the ark, feeding upon Christ as the hidden manna, partaking of Him as the budding rod, and experiencing the working of the law of life. As we have seen, the working of the law of life will make us the corporate reproduction of God's standard model for the fulfillment of His eternal purpose. All the paths from the altar in the outer court to the ark in the Holy of Holies are the way for us to have the fulfillment of God's economy and the enjoyment of the birthright. Ultimately, it is the way into perfection, glorification, and the full taste of God. Everything we need is on this way.

Once we are on this way, we should not linger or hesitate. We must run the race, forgetting Judaism, Christianity, and every other religion. As soon as we start to run on the way, it becomes a race composed of many paths. The path from the altar to the laver, from the laver to the showbread table, from the showbread table to the lampstand, from the lampstand to the incense altar, and from the incense altar to the ark—these are the paths which compose God's unique way.

Why do we need so many turns in Christ as the way? Because we need the cross to eliminate all the negative things in us. I have already pointed out that the arrangement of the furniture in the tabernacle forms the symbol of the cross. The way in Christ is in the shape of a cross. In fact, the way even is the cross. When we begin at the altar in the outer court, we are filled with many negative things, such as sin, the world, the flesh, lusts, and Satan. But as we move along the paths, making all the turns, these negative things are crossed out. Once we reach the ark in the Holy of Holies we are a purified person. I say again that all the negative things are crossed out by the turns which form the paths. What remains after making all these turns is a resurrected, uplifted humanity which is suitable to be mingled with divinity. How marvelous this is! Only God could have designed it.

Now we may come to the experiences of Christ in 13:8-15. Since so many things have been covered in the first twelve chapters of Hebrews, why does the writer include the experiences of Christ found in chapter thirteen? Because the Judaizers were using a certain aspect of their religious ceremonies—the eating of the festival food—to attract the Hebrew believers. According to the Old Testament, the children of Israel came to Jerusalem three times a year for the worship of God in their annual feasts, coming together to feast for several days. In these feasts they ate the festival food. This eating together, which was a very attractive thing, is the background of verse 9, which says, "Do not be carried away with various and strange teachings, for it is good for the heart to be confirmed by grace, not by foods, in which those who walked were not profited." The word "food" mentioned here is in contrast with "grace" and refers to the foods of the ceremonial observances of the old covenant (9:10; Col.

2:16) which the Judaizers used in their attempts to carry away the Hebrew believers from the enjoyment of grace, which is the participation in Christ in the new covenant.

At the time of their festivals, all the Israelites were excited, much more excited than Americans and Europeans are at Christmas time. It was very difficult for the seekers of Christ to stay away from such a charming attraction. The Judaizers might have come to the Hebrew believers, saying, "In a few days the feast of tabernacles will begin. If you don't go, you will lose all the enjoyment. Where will you be while we are singing, dwelling together, and enjoying all the riches of the good land? You will be assembling with that church in a little house. What will you have to eat there? If you go there, you will lose the right to kill the sacrifices for your eating. If you want to eat, you must go with us to the temple. But you have given up our precious feast. This means that you so-called Christians have lost all this enjoyment." If you were a Jew and had been there at the time, could you have withstood this attraction? Most of us would have been unable to resist. Then a fellow believer might have come to the Hebrew Christians, saying, "Don't go back to the temple. If you do, you will fall away from the grace of God. Don't listen to the strange teachings about the food in our old religion. Christ is the reality. He is everything." In the midst of such a dilemma, the Hebrew believers did not know what to do. Because of this, the writer gave them a strong word in chapter thirteen.

I. CHRIST BEING UNCHANGEABLE, REMAINING THE SAME FOREVER

Verse 8 says, "Jesus Christ is the same yesterday, and today, and forever." The Christ, who is the word which the ministers of the word of God in verse 7 preached and taught, who is the life which they lived, and who is the Author and Perfecter of their faith, is perpetual, unchangeable, and unchanging. He remains the same forever (1:11-12). The writer seemed to be telling the Hebrew believers, "Brothers, God sent His messengers to preach to you the word of

Christ. Christ was not only the word they preached, but the very life by which they lived. This Christ is always the same. He is the same yesterday, today, and forever. If you accepted Him as the Christ in the past, you should not change your concept now due to the strange teachings about eating. Do not sell your birthright in Christ for one meal of this ceremonial eating. If you had not received Christ, I would not speak to you this way. But you have received the unchangeable Christ. Since He does not change, you should not change either. Do not be distracted by the strange teachings about ceremonial eating. That eating means nothing." Hebrews is a deep book. We cannot understand it according to the black and white letters. If we would understand chapter thirteen, we must plunge into the depths of this book.

II. HOLDING ON TO THE UNCHANGEABLE CHRIST FOR A TRUE AND STEADFAST CHURCH LIFE

Verse 9 mentions "various and strange teachings." For a true and steadfast church life, we must hold on to the unchangeable Christ and not be carried away with various and strange teachings used by Satan to cause dissension and even division in the church. Because of the dissension and division caused by strange teachings, the apostle charged people "not to teach differently" (1 Tim. 1:3, Gk.). These various and strange teachings must have been taught by the Judaizers at that time. The writer warned the Hebrew believers not to let the teachings carry them away from the church life under the new covenant. There must not be "another Jesus," "another gospel," preached in the church (2 Cor. 11:4; Gal. 1:8-9). For a true and steadfast church life, we must hold on to the Christ who is the same yesterday, today, and forever, and not be carried away with various and strange teachings.

III. BEING CONFIRMED BY GRACE TO REMAIN IN THE NEW COVENANT TO ENJOY CHRIST AS GRACE

As the Judaizers used the foods of their ceremonial observances of the old covenant to distract the Hebrew believers, so the writer of this book charges the believers to be confirmed by grace. At that time, to be confirmed by grace was to remain in the new covenant to enjoy Christ as grace (Gal. 5:4) and not to be carried away to Judaism to participate in the eating of foods in the Jewish religious ceremonies.

Many dear ones have seen the Lord's recovery, but due to the matter of Christmas, they sold their birthright. Their Christmas celebration was like the religious meals in Judaism. Many American and European Christians find it difficult to give up Santa Claus and Christmas trees. The teachings about Christmas trees, Santa Claus, and stockings are some of today's various and strange teachings. A number of saints in the western world have been distracted from the Lord's recovery by these very things. If we would take away these things, many of the children would forsake the church, and many grandparents would be unhappy, saying, "Who is this preacher who comes to our country to take away Christmas, Santa Claus, and the Christmas stockings?" Others have said, "We know that the Lord's recovery is the way, but because our children cannot give up Christmas, we cannot take this way." In principle, they have been drawn away by today's religious attractions as the Hebrew believers were by the festival foods in the first century.

IV. THE CROSS BEING OUR ALTAR ON WHICH CHRIST OFFERED HIMSELF AS THE SIN OFFERING

Verse 10 says, "We have an altar, from which they have no right to eat who serve the tabernacle." This altar must be the cross on which the Lord Jesus offered Himself as the sacrifice for our sins (10:12). According to the regulations regarding the offerings in the Old Testament, the sacrifice for sin, or sin offering, whose blood was brought into the Holy of Holies or Holy Place for atonement, afforded nothing for the offering priest or the offerer to eat. The entire offering was burnt (Lev. 4:2-12; 16:27; 6:30). Hence, from the altar of the sin offering (which in the fulfillment of the New Testament is the Lord's cross) those who served the tabernacle have no right to eat. Verse 10 is a strong argument against the food used by the Judaizers in their strange teaching, attempting to carry away the new covenant believers from the enjoyment of Christ. As we have seen, their emphasis was on the food which they enjoyed in their religious services. But the writer of this book argues that in the sin offering, the basic offering for their yearly atonement (Lev. 16), there was nothing for anyone to eat. With the sin offering it is not a matter of eating, but of receiving its efficacy. Now the real sin offering is Christ, who has offered Himself to God for our sins and accomplished full redemption for us that we might be brought into the enjoyment of God's grace in Him under the new covenant. What we need today is not to eat the foods of the old covenant services, but to receive the efficacy of Christ's offering and follow Him in the new covenant grace outside the camp, outside the Jewish religion.

In this book Christ is presented only as the sin offering, not as any other offering. Since our problem with God is basically a problem of sin, the sin offering is the basic and most crucial of all the offerings. If our problem of sin had not been solved, our problem with God would still remain. Several times in this book we are told that Christ offered Himself (7:27; 9:14), but each time we see that Christ offered Himself as the sin offering. Thus, the argument in chapter thirteen is this: however much the Hebrew Christians went to the festivals to eat the ceremonial meals, they could not eat of the sin offering. But now they enjoy Christ as the sin offering. Of this offering there was nothing for those in Judaism to eat. Furthermore, verse 11 says, "The bodies of those animals, whose blood is brought into the Holy of Holies by the high priest concerning sin, are burned outside the camp." Christ's body was carried outside the gate. There He suffered death and, in a sense, was burned. As the sin offering, Christ is not for food but for sacrifice outside the gate.

V. CHRIST'S BODY SUFFERING THE DEATH OF THE CROSS OUTSIDE THE GATE AND HIS BLOOD BEING BROUGHT INTO THE HOLY OF HOLIES FOR OUR SANCTIFICATION

Verse 12 says, "Wherefore also Jesus, that He might sanctify the people through His own blood, suffered outside the gate." The blood of the sin offering being brought into the Holy of Holies on the day of atonement to make atonement for the people and its body being burnt outside the camp (Lev. 16:14-16, 27) typify the blood of Christ, the real sin offering, being brought into the true Holy of Holies to accomplish redemption for us and His body being sacrificed for us outside the gate of the city of Jerusalem.

Christ's body suffered the death of the cross outside the gate, and His blood was brought into the Holy of Holies for our sanctification (vv. 11-12). This book unveils that God's heavenly calling is to make us a heavenly people (3:1), a people who are sanctified unto God. Christ is the Sanctifier (2:11). He suffered the death of the cross, shed His blood on it, and entered the Holy of Holies with His blood (9:12) that He might be able to do the sanctifying work by the heavenly ministry (8:2, 6) of His heavenly priesthood (7:26), and that we might enter "within the veil" by His blood to participate in Him as the heavenly Sanctifier. By participating in Him in this way, we shall be enabled to follow Him outside the camp by the sanctifying pathway of the cross.

VI. GOING FORTH TO HIM "OUTSIDE THE CAMP" BEARING HIS REPROACH TO FOLLOW HIM IN THE SANCTIFYING PATHWAY OF THE CROSS

The Lord's blood, through which He entered into the Holy of Holies (9:12), has opened a new and living way for us to enter "within the veil" to enjoy Him in the heavens as the glorified One (10:9-20); and His body, which was sacrificed for us on the cross, cut the narrow way of the cross for us to go outside the camp to follow Him on earth as the suffering One. Verse 13 says, "Let us therefore go forth unto Him outside the camp, bearing His reproach." If we would be real Christians, we must experience Christ, not in the way of eating a religious meal, but in the way of going outside the camp to bear His reproach, following Him in the sanctifying pathway of the cross. We must experience Christ in this particular aspect. If we would experience Him in this aspect, we must enter "within the veil," that is, enter into the Holy of Holies, to enjoy Him as our heavenly Sanctifier in His heavenly priesthood (10:19-20; 6:19-20).

As we have pointed out, chapter thirteen covers many virtues needed for the church life. If we do not have these virtues, we cannot have the church life. Suppose the Hebrew believers had gone back to the temple to eat the ceremonial food. By doing that they would have been forsaking the experience of Christ as the One who was rejected by religion. If they had forsaken Christ in this aspect, returning to eat the ceremonial food in Judaism, it would have been impossible for them to have the church life. The principle is the same today. Those who have forsaken the church meetings and have returned to the religious practices in Christianity have given up their birthright. Those who have done this do not care for Christ and the church; they only care for today's religious attractions. Since they have sold their birthright, they can neither enjoy Christ nor exercise the priesthood and the kingship. Do you think that such believers will enjoy the birthright as the reward in the millennial kingdom? According to the clear revelation in the New Testament, if we do not exercise our spirit to remain in the church, enjoy Christ as our good land, and practice our priesthood and kingship today, we shall not deserve to enjoy our birthright as a reward in the millennial kingdom. If we would have the exercise of our birthright which will issue in receiving the reward in the kingdom, we must remain in the church.

In order to remain in the church, we must drop every religious practice. Some who have been pastors enjoy being called reverend, being unwilling to drop this title. Although only God is reverend (Psa. 111:9), they insist on keeping this title, enjoying it as their religious food. What profit is there in keeping such a title? If you keep it, you do so at the cost of your birthright. Our heart must be confirmed by grace, not by any religious food, that is, not by any religious attractions, positions, titles, and practices. We must forsake them all.

Grace is on the race, on the path. We should not be distracted from any path of this race, but continue on the race of grace. But many things are waiting for an opportunity to distract us from the paths of this race, that is, from the enjoyment of grace. As the arrangement of the furniture in the tabernacle reveals, every path of this race is an aspect of the enjoyment of Christ. We must keep on running this race in the enjoyment of Christ. Never be distracted by titles, positions, or religious attractions, all of which are merely religious "foods." We must experience Christ as our grace for the church life. If we do not experience Him in such a way, we cannot have the church life.

If we would experience Christ in this aspect, we must take the way of the cross, suffering persecution, rejection, and opposition from religion. Christ suffered outside the gate, and we must follow Him outside the gate to bear His reproach. If we share His suffering today, in the future we shall share in His glorification. If we experience Christ in this way, bearing His reproach on the pathway of the cross, we shall be kept in the rich church life, and every meeting of the church will be uplifted and enriched. In such a church life we shall be able to exercise our birthright. This will issue in our receiving the reward in the coming kingdom.

VII. HAVING HERE NO PERMANENT CITY, NO ORGANIZED REALM, BUT SEEKING THE COMING ONE, GOD'S HOLY CITY, THE NEW JERUSALEM

Verse 12 speaks of being "outside the gate," and verse 13 tells us to go "outside the camp." The gate here is the gate of the city of Jerusalem. The city signifies the earthly realm, and the camp signifies the human organization. The two signify one thing, the Jewish religion with its two aspects, the earthly and the human. Judaism is both earthly and human. Verse 14 says, "For here we do not have a permanent city, but we seek the coming one." This means that we do not have a permanent city, any organized realm, but we seek the coming one, God's Holy City, the New Jerusalem (Rev. 21:2, 10). By using the pronoun "we" in these verses the writer was considering himself and his readers as real river-crossing Hebrews like the patriarchs (11:9-10, 13-16).

VIII. IN THE HOLY OF HOLIES, OFFERING UP THROUGH HIM THE SACRIFICE OF PRAISE TO GOD

Verse 15 says, "Through Him then let us offer up a sacrifice of praise continually to God, that is, the fruit of lips confessing His name." This verse is a continuation of verses 8 through 14. Since in the church life we enjoy the unchanging Christ as grace and follow Him outside religion, we should offer up through Him spiritual sacrifices to God. Firstly, we should offer up through Him a sacrifice of praise continually to God in the church. In the church, He sings hymns of praise unto God the Father in us (2:12). We also should praise God the Father in the church through Him. Eventually He and we, we and He, will praise the Father in the church in the mingled spirit. He as the life-giving Spirit praises the Father in our spirit, and we, by our spirit, also praise the Father in His Spirit. This is the best and highest sacrifice we can offer to God through Him. This is greatly needed in the church meetings.

LIFE-STUDY OF HEBREWS

MESSAGE FIFTY-SEVEN

ENTER WITHIN THE VEIL AND GO OUTSIDE THE CAMP

If we get into the depths of the book of Hebrews, we shall see that the whole book is covered by two things—entering within the veil and going outside the camp. We must enter within the veil and go outside the camp. Within the veil there is one unique place—the Holy of Holies. When we are within the veil, we are within the Holy of Holies. In the Holy of Holies, the unique place, there is one unique thing—the ark of testimony, which is the full symbol of Christ. Inside this unique item are three precious things: the hidden manna, the budding rod, and the law of the testimony, that is, the law of life which issues in God's expression and testimony. This brief word, which opens a very wide field, tells us the meaning of the phrase "within the veil." To be within the veil is to be in the Holy of Holies, in a realm where we partake of Christ and enjoy the hidden manna, the budding rod, and the law of life which issues in God's corporate expression. This is the fulfillment of God's eternal purpose.

Hebrews 13:13 says, "Let us therefore go forth unto Him outside the camp, bearing His reproach." Both in this book and in typology the camp signifies the organization of religion, which is human and earthly. To go outside the camp means to go outside the human organization of religion. While the camp signifies the human organization, the city signifies the earthly realm. In the book of Hebrews, both the gate and the camp signify the Jewish religion with its two aspects, the earthly and the human. Judaism is both earthly and human. Every religion is both a human organization and an earthly realm which keeps people away from God's economy.

On the one hand, God's economy is being fulfilled within the veil. On the other hand, many religious things are taking place inside the camp. All we can see in the camp are just the religious things. Although many of the things in the camp may be related to the Bible, God is not there. Inside the camp, that is, in the organization of religion, there are no angels, church, Savior, saved ones, Christ, or sprinkled blood. Rather, there is a mountain set on fire producing a thick darkness and gloom, there is a whirlwind which moves without direction or peace, and there is the terrifying sound of a trumpet with the fearful words of warning. This is the picture of the Jewish religion as portrayed in this book. In all the foregoing messages we have seen a very vivid picture of what is within the veil on the one side and of the religious things in the camp on the other side. Now we all must choose where we shall be—within the veil or within the camp. We cannot be neutral.

The book of Hebrews instructs and charges us to come forward to the Holy of Holies and to enter within the veil. The way into the Holy of Holies, a new and living way, has been slain. Hence, this book firstly ushers us into the Holy of Holies and then directs us to go outside the camp. According to our mental figuration, we firstly go outside the camp and then enter within the veil. But this is our human mathematics. According to God's mathematics, we firstly enter within the veil and only then can we go outside the camp. Everyone who has gone outside the camp has firstly experienced what is within the veil. Perhaps when you began to come to the meetings of the church, you were not yet outside the camp. You were simply coming within the veil to have a taste. But that taste attracted you, caught you, and supplied you with the energy to go outside the camp. No one has firstly gone outside the camp and then entered within the veil. Although the Lord Jesus firstly went outside the gate and then entered within the veil, it is exactly the opposite with us. In other words, firstly we enter into the Holy of

Holies, where we are strengthened and encouraged to go outside the camp, and then we go out of the organization of religion. The more we enter within the veil, the more we go outside the camp.

I. THE HEAVENLY CHRIST WITHIN THE VEIL

The book of Hebrews firstly shows us the heavenly Christ who is within the veil, within the Holy of Holies (6:19-20). He is there as our High Priest (4:14; 7:26), as the heavenly Minister (8:2), and as the Mediator of the new covenant (8:6; 9:15; 12:24). As our High Priest, He is there interceding for us and ministering all the riches of God into us. As the heavenly Minister, He is carrying out His excellent ministry for us, and as the Mediator of the new covenant, He is executing all the contents of the new covenant for our enjoyment. All this is much better than what He did for us on earth while He was in the flesh.

II. THE BELIEVERS ENCOURAGED TO ENTER WITHIN THE VEIL

After showing us the heavenly Christ within the veil, the book of Hebrews encourages us to enter within the veil (10:19-20, 22). Within the veil, we can look away unto Him (12:2) and can consider Him (12:3; 3:1). We need to have direct contact with Him. Since He is within the veil, we also must enter within the veil that we may see Him, look at Him, and consider Him in order to receive the transfusion and infusion of Him. Of course, we can only do this by exercising our spirit. As we have seen, our spirit is joined to the heavenly Holy of Holies. When we turn to our spirit and exercise it, we enter within the veil. Here we participate in the heavenly ministry of the heavenly Christ. Here we are saturated and permeated with all the divine riches that make us the corporate reproduction of the Firstborn Son of God for His expression. Here we receive grace and are strengthened to go outside the camp and follow Him on the pathway of the cross.

III. THE BELIEVERS CHARGED TO GO OUTSIDE THE CAMP TO FOLLOW THE LORD

A. Moses Moving outside the Camp Where the Lord's Seekers Went to Meet with Him

After the children of Israel worshipped the golden calf (Exo. 32), Moses moved "without [outside] the camp," where everyone who sought the Lord went to meet with him, for both the Lord's presence and speaking were there (Exo. 33:7-11). Likewise, we must go outside the camp, wherein is the worship of the idol, that we may enjoy the Lord's presence and hear His speaking. This is necessary for the practical and proper church life.

B. Religion, Being a Camp Given Up by the Lord

The religion, either Judaism, Catholicism, or Protestantism, which has rejected the Lord, is a camp, a human organization, given up by the Lord. The great Babylon mentioned in Revelation 17 is even a worldly city, an earthly realm, from which the Lord's people must come out (Rev. 18:4).

The Devil has injected religion into our blood. Because of this, the camp is not merely outside of us; it is deep within us. Since the day Eve ate of the tree of the knowledge of good and evil, religion has been in man's blood. When the serpent tempted Eve, he did not ask her to do anything immoral. Rather, the serpent spoke to her in a religious way, saying, "Yea, hath God said, Ye shall not eat of every tree of the garden?" (Gen. 3:1). Here we see that the serpent even spoke of God. This is religion. The serpent seemed to be saying, "Eve, I know that you and your husband are both for God. I am not here to talk with you about worldly entertainments. I want to talk with you about God." Talking about God is an aspect of religion. Do you know what religion is? It is the mere talk about God. Some may say, "Isn't it wonderful that people talk about God? Why do you condemn them for this?

In religion people are taught to know God. Their subject is not fornication or gambling; it is the true God." Nevertheless, as Genesis 3 reveals, religion began with the serpent's talking to Eve about God. Eve answered the serpent, saying, "We may eat of the fruit of the trees of the garden: but of the fruit of the tree which is in the midst of the garden, God has said, Ye shall not eat of it, neither shall ye touch it, lest ye die" (Gen. 3:2-3). To this the serpent responded, "Ye shall not surely die: for God doth know that in the day ye eat thereof, then your eyes shall be opened, and ye shall be as gods, knowing good and evil" (Gen. 3:4-5). Knowing good and evil is also a matter of religion. Religion teaches people to know about God and to know good and evil. Eventually, Eve ate of the tree of knowledge, and religion was injected into man's blood.

There is no need for anyone to be taught religion; we all were born religious. This is the reason that whenever we preach in a religious way we are welcomed. But if we preach the gospel in the way of the Holy of Holies, the people will shout, "Crucify him!" as they did to the Lord Jesus. Because we were born and raised in religion, religion is not only in our concept, but also in our being, in our blood. Day after day we must go outside religion, outside the camp.

In a sense, religion closely resembles God's economy. In both the Old Testament and the New Testament we can find verses which seem to be for religion. But we must understand those verses in the light of the basic revelation of the Bible, which is the economy of God, the dispensing of God into man for His expression. God does not care for religion; He cares for His economy. He is for the dispensing of Himself into man. While God's intention is to work Himself into man, so many Christians only know their religion. They know nothing of God's economy, nor what it means to say that the Triune God is dispensed into our being. Having become a religion, Christianity is far off from God's economy. But we in the Lord's recovery do not care for anything religious. We just care for the dispensing of the Triune God into us.

C. Going Forth unto Jesus outside Religion, Bearing His Reproach

To be within the veil is to enter into the Holy of Holies where the Lord is enthroned in glory, and to go outside the camp is to come out of religion, whence the Lord was cast out in rejection. This signifies that we must be in our spirit, where, experientially speaking, the practical Holy of Holies is today, and outside religion, where the practical camp is today. The more we are in our spirit enjoying the heavenly Christ, the more we shall be outside religion following the suffering Jesus. To be in our spirit to enjoy the glorified Christ enables us to come outside religion to follow the rejected Jesus. The more we contact the heavenly Christ in His glory in our spirit, the more we shall go to the lowly Jesus in His suffering outside religion. To contact Christ in the heavens, enjoying His glorification, energizes us to take the narrow pathway of the cross on the earth and to bear His reproach. The book of Hebrews firstly gives us a clear vision of the heavenly Christ and the heavenly Holy of Holies, and then it shows us how to walk the pathway of the cross on the earth, that is, to go forth unto Jesus outside the camp, outside religion, bearing His reproach. To go forth unto Jesus outside the camp, bearing His reproach, is to take the pathway of the cross.

D. The Holy of Holies Enabling Us to Take the Pathway of the Cross and the Pathway of the Cross Ushering Us into the Kingdom

The Holy of Holies, the pathway of the cross (signified by going forth unto Jesus outside the camp, bearing His reproach), and the kingdom are three crucial matters set forth in this book. The Holy of Holies enables us to take the pathway of the cross, and the pathway of the cross ushers us into the kingdom in its manifestation. To enter into the kingdom in its manifestation we need to take the pathway of the cross, and to take the pathway of the cross we need to enter into the Holy of Holies within the veil. The Holy of Holies is crucial to our Christian walk.

IV. TO ENTER WITHIN THE VEIL IS TO GET INTO OUR SPIRIT

If we would enter within the veil, we must get into our spirit (4:12). To be within the veil is to be in our spirit, and to be outside the camp is to be outside anything religious. We must not remain in any camp, but get into our spirit. If you remain in the religious camp, you are still camping outside your spirit. But we are no longer camping—we are in the Holy of Holies. The writer seemed to be telling the Hebrew believers, "Brothers, get out of your camping mind and get into your spirit." Today we also must exercise to bring our whole being into the spirit. We must not remain in our camping mentality, for that mentality is religious. Again and again we need to enter within the veil by entering into our spirit.

It is difficult for Christian readers to understand why the writer of Hebrews mentions the spirit in 4:12. As he is comparing Christ with Judaism, he suddenly says, "The word of God is living and operative and sharper than any two-edged sword, and piercing even to the dividing of soul and spirit." Now we understand that this verse shows us the key to experiencing Christ—our spirit which is joined to the Holy of Holies. Therefore, we must discern our spirit from our camping mentality, from our camping soul. We must no longer camp in our mind but turn to our spirit. The Lord Jesus Christ is with our spirit (2 Tim. 4:22). Grace is with our spirit (Gal. 6:18). We have seen that we must take grace, but where do we go to take grace? We must go to our spirit. The Holy of Holies, God's economy, and even the fulfillment of God's economy are all related to our spirit. What we need today is to enter within the veil by getting into the spirit.

Suppose some young brothers are fighting with one another. This is a type of wild camping. But do not think they need some religious ones to tell them to behave themselves, to learn patience, and to camp religiously. That would merely be to teach them how to camp in their religious soul. This is not to enter within the veil. The brothers who are fighting with one another need to turn to their spirit. Once they turn to the spirit and take grace, they will taste Christ as their hidden manna, partake of Him as the budding rod, and experience the regulating of the law of life. Then they will not need anyone to teach them patience, humility, or the lesson of giving in.

God's economy is the dispensation of the Triune God into our being. This builds up the Body of Christ, producing material for the building up of the church. This transpires in the Holy of Holies within the veil, which is joined to our spirit. What a difference between this and religion! If we experience Christ in such an inner way, we shall see how much of the religious camping element is still in our blood. Spontaneously, we shall begin to hate this religious element and loathe our camping self. We all need to enter within the veil that the Lord may bring us into such a realization.

If we are faithful to the Lord and enter within the veil day after day and week after week, we shall discover that much of our religious background still remains within us. The brothers with a Jewish background will find that the Jewish religious element is still in them, and those with a Presbyterian or Southern Baptist background will discover that those camping elements remain in their blood. Many times in the past you have probably measured or estimated the condition of the church life by your religious background, comparing the church life with that camping element. But the more we enter within the veil and are transfused and infused with the heavenly Christ, the more we shall say, "Religious background, get away from me!" Nevertheless, although it seems that we have cast out the camping element, some of it still clings to us. Therefore, we need to continue to enter within the veil and go outside the camp.

A very touchy camping element is the matter of tongue speaking. Those who have had a tongue-speaking background often ask, "What about tongue speaking in the church?

Where do you put this? Do you think that it is useless?" Perhaps you have asked such questions many times. How difficult it is to leave our religious background! I am not condemning tongue speaking. We are for anything that is for God's economy, for the dispensing of the Triune God into us for the building up of the Body of Christ. We are not for any kind of religion, whether it is fundamental, Pentecostal, or charismatic. We are for just one thing—the dispensation of the Triune God into our being that we might be transformed and built together as His corporate expression and that we might terminate this age and usher in the kingdom. This can only be accomplished by our entering within the veil to experience the ark of God's testimony with the hidden manna, the budding rod, and the law of life. By experiencing these things, we are infused, empowered, strengthened, and enabled to go outside of every camp. My real burden in all these messages on Hebrews is that we may all enter within the veil and go outside the camp. This is the goal and the ultimate conclusion of this book.

When we enter within the veil by getting into our spirit, we taste the sweetness of the heavenly Christ that we may be enabled to go outside the camp, forsaking the earth and its love. As we stay within the veil, we also have our spirit filled with the glory of the heavenly Christ that our heart may be freed from the possession of the earth's enjoyment outside the camp. Furthermore, within the veil we behold the glorified Christ that we may be attracted to follow the suffering Jesus outside the camp. Beholding His countenance in heaven enables us to trace His footsteps on earth. As we enter within the veil, we are infused with resurrection power (Phil. 3:10) that we may be empowered to walk the pathway of the cross outside the camp. We also participate in the ministry of the heavenly Christ that we may be equipped to minister Him to the thirsty spirits outside the camp. Here we enjoy the Lord's best that we may be enriched to meet the needs of people outside the camp.

V. BEING EQUIPPED IN EVERY GOOD WORK BY ENTERING WITHIN THE VEIL AND GOING OUTSIDE THE CAMP

Verses 20 and 21 say, "Now the God of peace Who brought up from among the dead our Lord Jesus, the great Shepherd of the sheep, by the blood of an eternal covenant, equip you in every good work for the doing of His will, doing in us that which is well-pleasing in His sight through Jesus Christ, to Whom be the glory forever and ever, Amen." By entering within the veil and going outside the camp we are equipped in every good work. In this way God is doing in us that which is well-pleasing in His sight through Jesus Christ. He is doing this that we may be able to do His will. God "works in us both to will and to do of His good pleasure" (Phil. 2:13). From beginning to end, this book presents to us a heavenly Christ. Only here, with the word "doing in us that which is well-pleasing in His sight," does this book imply the indwelling of Christ. It is through the indwelling Christ whom we enjoy within the veil in our spirit that God works in us that we may do His will.

In verse 20 the Lord Jesus is spoken of as being the "great Shepherd of the sheep." The "sheep" here are the flock which is the church. This confirms the understanding that everything covered in this chapter is for the church life with the experience of the unchanging Christ as our sin offering, through whom we have been redeemed, and as our great Shepherd, by whom we are now being fed.

Verse 20 also speaks of an "eternal covenant." Hebrews is not a book concerning temporal things, such as the things of the old covenant; it is a book of eternal things, things which are beyond the limit of time and space, such as eternal salvation (5:9), eternal judgment (6:2), eternal redemption (9:12), eternal Spirit (9:14), eternal inheritance (9:15), and eternal covenant (13:20). The new covenant is not only a better covenant (7:22; 8:6), but also an eternal covenant. It is eternally effective because of the eternal efficacy of Christ's blood with which it was enacted (Matt. 26:28; Luke 22:20).

This book closes with the word of blessing, "Grace be with you all. Amen." If we would realize and participate in all the things unveiled in this book, we need grace. To take grace (12:28) we need to come forward to the throne of grace that we may find grace for our timely need (4:16). It is by touching the throne of grace in the Holy of Holies through the exercise of our spirit that we enjoy the Spirit of grace (10:29) and that our heart is confirmed by grace (13:9). By such an enjoyment of grace we run the race which is set before us (12:1) to reach the goal of God's economy.

LIFE-STUDY OF HEBREWS

MESSAGE FIFTY-EIGHT

EATING AND MANNA

In this message we come to the manna in the golden pot (9:4).

EATING, A BASIC MATTER IN THE BIBLE

If we would understand what the hidden manna, the manna in the golden pot, is, we must understand a basic concept in the Bible, a concept which most Christians have not grasped. After God created man, He did not do anything with him, nor did He charge him to do anything for Him. According to Genesis 1 and 2, the basic requirement for living in the presence of God is to eat properly. What matters the most in God's presence is what and how we eat. Hence, in the Bible eating is a basic concept concerning our relationship with God. God has created everything, including man. If He can make the heavens and the earth and billions of items, what is there that He cannot do? He can easily do everything. Actually, there is even no need for Him to do anything, for He just speaks and what He desires comes into being. Nevertheless, there is one thing which God cannot do—He cannot eat for us. Although a mother may do many things for her children, she cannot eat for them. The children must eat for themselves. As far as our relationship with God is concerned, the basic matter is eating properly.

EATING FOR THE SUPPLY OF LIFE AND FOR REDEMPTION

In Genesis 2, man's eating was a matter of the tree of life. After man fell, God came in to redeem him. But when God brought in redemption in Exodus 12, the eating was changed to include more than just the one item, the tree of life. Eating was no longer simply to have the supply of life; it was also related to redemption. In Exodus 12 the children of Israel were instructed to eat a lamb. The tree of life is of the vegetable life, and a lamb is of the animal life. While there is no blood with a tree, there is blood with a lamb. In the Bible, blood is for redemption. At the time of the exodus, the children of Israel struck the blood that they might be redeemed and they ate the lamb that they might have the life supply. In the first stage, eating was only for man's life supply, but in the second stage, eating was for both redemption and the life supply.

EATING THE LORD'S FLESH AND DRINKING HIS BLOOD

During the years in the wilderness, the children of Israel ate manna. Since there certainly was no blood in the manna, the eating of manna was unrelated to redemption; it was altogether for the life supply. How could the children of Israel, who wandered in the wilderness for forty years, continue to live and move? They lived and moved by the supply of manna which they ate every day. In chapter six of John, the Lord Jesus said, "I am the bread of life" (v. 35). This troubled the Jews. Then the Lord said, "Unless you eat the flesh of the Son of Man and drink His blood, you have no life in yourselves" (v. 53, Recovery Version). In this chapter the Lord firstly said that He was the bread of life. Then He said that we must drink His blood. How could the bread have blood in it? This bread is not only the bread of the vegetable life but also the meat of the lamb. In John 6:51 the Lord said, "The bread which I will give is My flesh, which I will give for the life of the world" (Recovery Version). The bread is of the vegetable life and is only for feeding; the flesh is of the animal life and is not only for feeding but also for redeeming. Before the fall of man, the Lord was the tree of life (Gen. 2:9), only for feeding man. After man fell into sin, the Lord became the Lamb (John 1:29), not only for feeding man, but also for redeeming him (Exo. 12:4, 7-8).

THE NEED TO KEEP EATING

I want to say again that after the creation of man and even in God's redemption of man, the basic concept regarding our being in the presence of God is this matter of eating. Thus, we must devote our complete attention to it. Do not try to learn so many things—just continue to eat well in the presence of the Lord. I was a Christian for over thirty years before I knew anything about eating in the spirit. I was never taught about this. Many of us can testify that before we came into the church, we were never told that we could eat Jesus. But from beginning to end, the Bible covers the matter of eating. The Bible begins and ends with the eating of the tree of life (Rev. 2:7, 22:1-2, 14).

EATING IN THE BOOK OF HEBREWS

As we have pointed out, the entire book of Hebrews is focused on Christ as the heavenly Minister with His kingly and divine priesthood. As our heavenly Minister, His main responsibility is to minister the Triune God into us as our supply. He is now ministering such a wonderful supply, not in the outer court, but in the Holy of Holies, and not on the cross, but on the throne of grace. We have seen that the book of Hebrews calls us to come forward to the Holy of Holies, to the throne of grace, and to God. In the Holy of Holies we are not gathered around the cross for redemption; we are meeting around the throne of grace for the life supply. Here we enjoy Christ as our Melchisedec ministering to us the bread and wine as our life supply. This also is absolutely a matter of eating. Hence, this book brings us from the outer court to the Holy of Holies, where there is one unique item—the ark of testimony, which represents Christ. In the Holy of Holies there is nothing but the all-inclusive Christ. According to the outward appearance, He is only one item, the ark of testimony. But when we experience Him as the ark, we see not only one unique item; we see three items—the golden pot containing manna, the budding rod, and the law of life.

These three items are the kernels within the kernel. After entering into the tabernacle, we find ourselves in the Holy Place where everything is rather outward. After passing through the second veil, we enter into the inner chamber of the tabernacle called the Holy of Holies. Once we have come into the Holy of Holies, we are in the heart, the kernel, of the tabernacle. But within the Holy of Holies we have the ark of testimony, and within the ark we have the golden pot containing manna, the budding rod, and the law of life. Because these items are all in the ark in the Holy of Holies, we may say that they are the kernels within the kernel.

As we touch the first of these items, the golden pot containing manna, we find something even deeper. After passing through four layers, the layer of the tabernacle, the layer of the Holy of Holies, the layer of the ark of testimony, and the layer of the golden pot, we come to the manna. When we touch this, we have truly come home. If we are only in the Holy of Holies but are not feeding on the manna in the golden pot, we are not yet home. Even if we touch the ark of testimony, we are still not home. The tabernacle is for the Holy of Holies, the Holy of Holies is for the ark, the ark is for the golden pot, and the golden pot is for the hidden manna. In Revelation 2:17 the Lord Jesus said, "To him that overcometh will I give to eat of the hidden manna." Where is this hidden manna? It is in the golden pot which is in the ark in the Holy of Holies. The one main kernel, the living kernel among all the kernels, is the hidden manna. The Lord Jesus promised His overcomers that they would eat this hidden manna.

THE MEANING OF MANNA

Before we learn how to eat the hidden manna, we must first know what manna is. The word manna means "What is this?" (Exo. 16:15). The manna which the children of Israel ate in the wilderness was different from the other foods they had known, for it was unlike any food stuff on earth. It was neither wheat, corn, nor barley. When the people saw it, they asked, "What is this?" In Numbers 11 we see a comparison between manna and the foods with which the children of Israel were familiar. Numbers 11:5-6 says, "We remember the fish, which we did eat in Egypt freely; the cucumbers, and the melons, and the leeks, and the onions, and the garlic: but now our soul is dried away: there is nothing at all, beside this manna, before our eyes." Here we see the leeks, the onions, and the garlic. Although the children of Israel knew what these were, they did not know what manna was. In color, shape, appearance, taste, and in every other aspect it was absolutely different from anything they had ever seen before. They could only ask, "What is this?" They seemed to be saying, "What is this? It is neither fish nor leeks, onions nor garlic. Is it animal or vegetable? It seems that it is neither one." No human language can explain what manna is. Manna is simply manna. Manna is "What is this?" Everyone knows what onions are, but when you speak of manna they can only ask "What is this?" Manna is simply "What is this?"

Manna is a type of Christ. What is Christ? Christ is "What is this?" He is extraordinary. He is so special that He cannot be ranked with anything else.

THE VARIOUS ASPECTS OF MANNA

Coming with the Dew

Let us now consider the various aspects of the manna in the Old Testament. Numbers 11:9 says, "When the dew fell upon the camp in the night, the manna fell upon it." Manna always comes early in the morning with the dew. What does the dew signify? Psalm 133:3 says, "As the dew of Hermon, and as the dew that descended upon the mountains of Zion." In the Bible, dew signifies God's gracious visitation from the heavens. When God comes from the heavens to visit us as grace, He is like the dew, so precious and watering. That manna always comes with the dew signifies that the very Christ who is our manna today always comes with grace, with God's gracious visitation from the heavens. Whenever we touch Christ as our life supply, we have the deep sense that heaven has come to us in a soft, watering manner. This watering is so well proportioned that it does not trouble us, but it certainly refreshes us. As we enjoy touching Christ as our manna, we have the sense that heaven has come down to visit, water, and refresh us.

Small

Exodus 16:14 describes manna as "a small round thing, as small as the hoar frost on the ground." Although some hymns have been written to praise Christ for His greatness, we also need to praise Him for His smallness. Manna was small; yet the Bible does not give us its dimensions. Although manna is small, it is immeasurable; we cannot say how small it is. This indicates that we cannot tell the size of Christ. Our Christ is without size. Nothing is smaller than He is, and nothing is greater than He is. He is the smallest as well as the greatest. Nothing can exceed Him. Who can measure the greatness or the smallness of Christ?

Round

We are also told that the manna was round (Exo. 16:14). In typology, this signifies that manna is eternal, without beginning or ending. Christ is the eternal food with the eternal nature for the eternal nourishment without any limitation. Whoever eats Him will have the eternal life with the eternal nature and receive the eternal nourishment.

Like the Frost

Manna was like the frost (Exo. 16:14), which is between dew and snow. Dew is refreshing, but it is not as refreshing as frost is. Although dew refreshes, it does not kill the germs. Frost does kill germs. As manna, Christ not only refreshes us; He also kills all the negative things within us. He comes with the dew, and He comes as the frost. Whenever we experience Christ as the supply, we sense that heaven has come down to visit and water us. While we are being watered and refreshed, we also sense that the negative things within us, such as our negative attitudes, are being killed. I enjoy the refreshing and the killing of this frost. If two brothers are upset with one another, it means that they need the killing of the frost.

The frost not only kills the negative things in us; it also cools us down. Although the young people love the Lord, sometimes they are "hot" for sports. If they do not have the time to go to a football game, they may at least try to watch a game on television. When, while they are so "hot" for sports, they touch Christ, the "frost" will come to cool them down. Other brothers and sisters like to talk, talking in vain words about many things. When we talk like this, we are "hot." But when we touch Christ, the "frost" cools us down. The older brothers and sisters also need to be cooled down by the "frost." Although the older sisters love their husbands, if we would ask the husbands to speak frankly, they would say that they cannot stand the bothering of their wives. Neither can the older sisters bear the bothering of their retired husbands. Many of the retired brothers have little to do every day except to bother their wives. By this we see that even the older ones need to be cooled down. The older we are, the more bothersome we are. Hence, we all need the "frost" to cool down our hot temper. In a sense, this "frost" is our spiritual refrigerator. The very Christ within us who nourishes us is also the frost which freezes us.

White

The manna in the wilderness was white (Exo. 16:31). This means that it was clean and pure. No earthly food is as white as manna. Manna is the purest food. The more we feast on Christ, eating of Him as our manna, the more we are whitened. We are not only cleansed and purified; we are whitened. To be white means to be absolutely without stain. As we feed on Christ, all our stains are eliminated. Although we may be good in certain respects, we are not white. Although we may be loving, our love is not white; it is colored. Our humility is also colored. In fact, none of our human attributes is white; every one of them is colored. But the more we take in Christ as our life supply, the more our color will be reduced and the whiter we shall become.

An excellent Chinese food is sea cucumber. But because it is black in color, the American brothers are unwilling to eat it. Although I have tried my best to convince them to eat it, they are all afraid of its black appearance. Manna, on the contrary, is white and does not frighten anyone. Rather, it gives us the feeling of peace.

Eaten as Bread, Cakes, and Wafers

The manna was eaten as bread (Exo. 16:15), as cakes (Num. 11:8), and as wafers (Exo. 16:31). As our manna, Christ has different aspects and nourishes us in different ways. When we eat Him as our manna, sometimes He tastes like bread and at other times He tastes like a cake or like a wafer which is thin and easy to eat and digest.

Like a Coriander Seed

The manna was also like coriander seed (Exo. 16:31; Num. 11:7). This food is a seed. When we eat Christ, He comes into us as a seed. The coriander seed, unlike corn, is very tiny. A seed is something of life which brings the life element into our being. As such a seed, Christ will grow within us.

With the Taste of Honey

In Exodus 16:31 we are told that the taste of manna was like wafers made with honey. Honey is sweet and is the produce of two lives, the animal life and the vegetable life. Honey is the mingling of these two lives. The honey bees which produce honey receive the supply from flowers, from the vegetable life. As our manna, Christ has this element of the mingling of the animal life with the vegetable life which becomes our sweet nourishment.

As the Taste of Fresh Oil

Numbers 11:8 says of the manna that "the taste of it was as the taste of fresh oil." Oil typifies the Holy Spirit. When we eat Christ as our manna, we taste the Spirit of God. The oil here is the fresh oil. The Spirit we taste when we enjoy Christ as manna is always fresh. As our manna, Christ tastes like fresh oil and has the flavor and nourishment of honey.

With the Appearance of Bdellium

According to the original Hebrew, Numbers 11:7 says, "The manna was as coriander seed, and the eye thereof as the eye of bdellium." It is difficult for anyone to translate this verse properly. The King James Version says that the color was as the color of bdellium. Bdellium is a pearl produced by the resin from a tree and is very much like the pearl produced by an oyster. The color of manna is the color of bdellium. Other versions use the word appearance instead of color. However, the Hebrew word here is eye. Manna has an eye, for its appearance is like that of an eye. A pearl somewhat resembles an eye. If you examine a pearl, you will see that it is like an eyeball. An eyeball has the appearance of pearl, and this appearance is its color. In other words, the appearance and color of bdellium are like an eye.

When we eat the manna, we eat many eyes, and all these eyes get into us. As the manna, Christ resembles an eye. The more we eat of Christ, the more eyes we shall have. The four living creatures in Revelation 4:6 are "full of eyes before and behind." At the front and at the rear, within and without, they are full of eyes. If you go to a greenhouse, you will see that none of the walls is opaque; every side is transparent. An eye means transparency. With the exception of our eyes, which are transparent, our whole body is opaque. If we do not have Christ, we do not have any eyes, and we are absolutely opaque. When we were saved, we began to be transparent. Now the more we enjoy Christ, the more transparent we become. Whenever we are with a brother who truly enjoys Christ, we can sense that he is transparent. Standing before him is like being in a transparent greenhouse. However, anyone who is not in the enjoyment of the Lord is altogether opaque. If you are with four such persons, you will feel like you are in a dungeon surrounded by opaque walls. But if you are surrounded by several brothers who love the Lord and feed on Him, you will sense that everything is transparent. As the manna, Christ is transparent. When we eat Him, we eat eyeballs and we become transparent.

This transparency will eventually become our appearance. If we enjoy Christ day after day, eating Him as the eyeball, we shall have the appearance of Christ, the appearance of an eyeball, and this appearance will become our color. By eating Christ, we are colored with the transparency of Christ. In this way, transparency becomes our appearance and color.

Not Legal

Finally, as the manna, Christ is not legal. Numbers 11:8 says, "The people went about, and gathered it, and ground it in mills, or beat it in a mortar, and baked it in pans, and made cakes of it." Christ can be ground, beaten in a mortar, or baked in pans. He is not legal. Nearly every Christian, however, is legal. If you experience Christ in a certain way, you make that a legal way. But Christ would say, "To you, I am ground. But others prefer to beat Me. I feel quite good when I am beaten in this way. Still others bake Me and put Me into an oven. I also feel good about this. Why are you so narrow and legal?"

What a wonderful record we find in the Bible regarding the manna. If we are asked what it is, we must simply say that it is manna. It comes with the dew and is like the frost on the ground. It is small, round, white, and like a coriander seed. It can be eaten as bread, cake, and wafers, it has the taste of honey and fresh oil, and its appearance is like an eyeball. Although we might have read Exodus 16 and Numbers 11 many times, we probably have never noticed all these aspects of the manna. We need to eat more eyeballs that we may have the transparent sight.

LIFE-STUDY OF HEBREWS

MESSAGE FIFTY-NINE

THE MANNA IN THE GOLDEN POT

In the last message we laid the foundation for knowing the manna. In this message we need to consider the hidden manna, the manna in the golden pot.

GOD'S COMMANDMENT REGARDING THE MANNA

The term hidden manna is used in Revelation 2:17, where the Lord Jesus says, "To him that overcometh will I give to eat of the hidden manna." This word was spoken to the church in Pergamos, a degraded, worldly church. If anyone overcomes degraded Christianity, the Lord will give him the hidden manna. Nearly everything mentioned in the book of Revelation, including the manna, can be found in the Old Testament. Exodus 16:32 and 33, referring to the manna, say, "Moses said, This is the thing which the Lord commandeth, Fill an omer of it to be kept for your generations; that they may see the bread wherewith I have fed you in the wilderness, when I brought you forth from the land of Egypt. And Moses said unto Aaron, Take a pot, and put an omer full of manna therein, and lay it up before the Lord, to be kept for your generations." The Lord commanded that an omer of manna be put into a pot. An omer is "the tenth part of an ephah" (Exo. 16:36). An ephah is a complete unit, and an omer is one tenth of a unit. This small portion was put into a pot and laid up before the testimony to be kept (Exo. 16:34). In Exodus, the testimony means the two tables of the law which were put into the ark. The omer of manna was put in front of the testimony, meaning that it was quite close to the ark. This portion of the manna became the hidden manna.

Manna came from heaven, from God, as a gift to His

people. It was not a temporary gift; it was a gift lasting for forty years. Morning after morning, this gift came down from heaven to feed and satisfy the children of Israel. After they had been satisfied, God seemed to say, "Take an omer of what you have enjoyed and put it before Me as a testimony and a reminder that the coming generations may be reminded that you enjoyed this heavenly food as you wandered in the wilderness." The open manna, the people's portion, came from God, and the hidden manna, God's portion, was offered back to God.

THE TITHE OF THE PRODUCE OF THE LAND

Now we need to consider the tithe, the basic concept of one tenth of the produce. The children of Israel were required to take the top tenth, the choicest portion of their produce in the good land, and offer it to God (Deut. 14:22-23). All the produce came from God. God ordained that one tenth of the produce which He had given the children of Israel be offered back to Him. The majority of the produce was for the people, but the tithe was offered to God as His portion. The tithe which was offered to God went to the priests and the Levites (Num. 18:21) who in turn took a tenth of the tithe they received and offered it to God. This tenth of the tenth went to the high priest who ministered in the Holy of Holies (Num. 18:26, 28-29). I repeat, the children of Israel offered one tenth of their produce to God as His portion. After this had been offered to God, it was given to the serving ones, to the priests and Levites who served the tabernacle. The priests and the Levites then took one tenth of this top tenth and offered it to God. It was then given to the high priest who ministered in the Holy of Holies. The Levites who served in the outer court and the priests who served in the outer court and in the Holy Place could only enjoy the tenth offered by the children of Israel. Only the high priest who served in the Holy of Holies was privileged to enjoy the tenth of the tenth, the topmost portion of the produce of the good land. Thus, the more we serve, the more we shall enjoy the topmost portion, God's portion.

THE HIDDEN MANNA BEING GOD'S PORTION

When the children of Israel were wandering in the wilderness, God gave them manna from heaven as a gift every day (except the Sabbath day). They all enjoyed this gift of manna. Then God seemed to say, "Take a portion, one tenth of an ephah, of the manna I have given you and place it before My testimony." This portion of the manna was for God. The open manna was the people's portion, and this offered, hidden manna in the pot before God's testimony was God's portion. The principle was the same with offering the produce after the children of Israel had entered into the good land. Once they were in the land, God no longer sent manna from heaven, for the good land provided all that was needed for their living. Thus, instead of gathering the manna, they harvested the produce of the good land. Regarding this, God seemed to say, "Give Me as My portion a tenth of all the produce you have harvested." The children of Israel did so, giving this one tenth to the priests and the Levites who served in and around the tabernacle. Then God told the priests and the Levites to take one tenth of what they received from the people and offer it to God. This portion, which we may call the top of the top, was then given to the high priest as his portion. Only the high priest, the one serving in the Holy of Holies, was privileged to enjoy this topmost portion.

Based upon this principle, we see that the hidden manna is the portion for God. The basic concept of the hidden manna is that it is God's portion. In the past, I was troubled whenever I read Exodus 16:36, which says, "Now an omer is the tenth part of an ephah." I thought that this verse was unnecessary and wondered why Moses included it. I could not understand the significance of an omer of manna being placed in a pot and put in front of the testimony of God. But just recently the Lord enlightened me about this, and I saw that the tenth is the choice portion, the portion for God.

Manna signifies Christ whom God has given to us as a gift. While we are enjoying Christ as our manna, we must take the best portion and offer it to God, offering Christ to God.

If we would eat the hidden manna, we must firstly eat the open manna. If we do not experience the open manna, we shall have no manna to offer God as the hidden manna. The hidden manna is the very manna which we experience, enjoy, and then offer to God. Eventually, because we are so intimate with God, He will say, "Come into My dining room and dine with Me." Do not think that you will suddenly enjoy Christ as your hidden manna if you have never enjoyed Him as your open manna. No, the hidden manna comes out of our enjoyment of the open manna. We enjoy manna and, out of the manna we enjoy, we offer a small portion to God, saying, "God, I offer to You the very Christ whom I have been enjoying. You have given Christ to me as my portion, and now I give the best of Him to You as Your portion." To this God will say, "Child, come into My Holy of Holies and enjoy this portion with Me." This is the hidden manna.

Let us consider our experience. When we enjoy Christ in a general way as our daily supply, we spontaneously desire to offer the very Christ whom we have enjoyed back to God, saying, "O God, how I thank You for the Christ whom You have given me. I have enjoyed Him very much. Now I would like to offer the best portion of Him to You." This is the omer of manna, the choice portion of the manna which is offered back to God. This portion is not for all of God's people; it is only for those who serve Him in a very intimate way in the Holy of Holies. This is the hidden manna, which comes out of the manna we enjoy in a general way.

Again I say that God has given us Christ as our food. As we enjoy Him as food, we gratefully offer Him back to God. In this way Christ becomes the choice portion of our enjoyment which we offer to God as His portion. God is pleased with this, accepts it, and says, "Since you are now with Me in the Holy of Holies, not serving Me in the outer court or in the Holy Place, I would like to serve you with what you have offered to Me. I ask you to enjoy the choicest portion of

Christ with Me." How wonderful this is! It closely matches both our experience and the whole revelation of the Bible and fits in with Revelation 2:17. Enjoying Christ as our hidden manna is not a sudden experience; it must have a history behind it.

HIDDEN BENEATH SEVERAL LAYERS

The hidden manna was hidden under at least four layers. Among the children of Israel was the tabernacle, within the tabernacle was the Holy of Holies, within the Holy of Holies was the ark, and within the ark was the golden pot. Anyone who wanted to enjoy the hidden manna firstly had to be among the children of Israel. Secondly, he had to enter into the tabernacle. Then he had to enter into the Holy of Holies. After that, he had to get into the ark containing the golden pot in which was the hidden manna.

Applying this to our situation today, we see that outside the church life it is impossible to enjoy the hidden manna. In the church life we have the various service groups. But these service groups, being the Levitical service, are only in the outer court. Nevertheless, by this outer court service, we are ushered into the Holy Place. Through the Holy Place we enter into the Holy of Holies. As many of us can testify, before we joined a service group, we were not even in the outer court; we were on the street. But as we serve with others, we have the sense that we are in the Holy Place enjoying Christ. Through this enjoyment we enter into the Holy of Holies where the hidden manna is.

THREE STAGES OF EATING IN THE TABERNACLE

In the tabernacle there are three stages of eating: eating the sacrifices around the altar, eating the showbread in the Holy Place, and eating the hidden manna in the golden pot in the Holy of Holies. Enjoying Christ at the altar ushers us into the Holy Place, where we enjoy Him in a finer way. The showbread on the table is much finer than the sacrifices on the altar. This is not merely a doctrine; it can be proved by our experience. As we enjoy Christ as our showbread, we experience something still different and say, "I am in the Holy of Holies eating something which I have never experienced before." This is the hidden manna.

THE HEAVE OFFERING

In the Old Testament there were two special offerings—the wave offering signifying the resurrected Christ and the heave offering signifying the uplifted, ascended Christ (Exo. 29:26-28). The tenth of the tenth which was offered to God for Aaron was a heave offering (Num. 18:28). As we experience Christ in the outer court and in the Holy Place, we enjoy not only the wave Christ but also the heave Christ, not only the resurrected Christ, but also the uplifted, exalted Christ. This means that eventually we shall be in the Holy of Holies enjoying the special portion of Christ hidden in God.

HIDDEN IN THE DIVINE NATURE

We have seen that Revelation 2:17 says that the Lord will give the overcomers to eat of the hidden manna. Colossians 3:3 says that our life is hid with Christ in God. Christ is hidden in God. The hidden manna mentioned in Revelation 2:17 was hidden in a golden pot (Heb. 9:4). In the Bible, gold signifies the divine nature. Hence, the hidden manna in the golden pot signifies the topmost portion of Christ hidden within the divine nature. The divine nature is in the ark, and, as we have seen, the ark is just Christ. This ark today is in our spirit, which is joined to the Holy of Holies. In our spirit we have the Holy of Holies, in the Holy of Holies we have Christ, the ark, and within Christ we have the golden pot, the divine nature. Here, within the divine nature, is the hidden manna. What is the hidden manna? It is Christ as our special portion of food hidden in the divine nature. When we are in the place where we touch the golden pot, we are absolutely outside the world, our self, and our natural man. We are touching the divine nature, and in the divine nature we partake of the hidden manna.

I ask you to check with your experience. After joining a service group, you were ushered into more of the church life and you began to experience something finer. Eventually, you were close to God and became intimate with Him. On some occasions, you were so close to God that you were beyond the world, your self, and even your natural being. You were another person with God in His nature. As you touched the divine nature, you touched the golden pot and enjoyed the manna hidden within it, enjoying Christ as your hidden portion in the divine nature.

As we shall see, the budding rod comes after the hidden manna, and the law of life follows the budding rod. These three crucial items, the contents of the ark, are arranged in such a sequence. Firstly, we must enjoy the hidden manna. Then out of our enjoyment of the hidden manna our rod will bud, and after that we shall have the law of life. Because so few Christians experience the hidden manna, their rod does not bud, and we very rarely find one who lives by the law of life. They do not understand the record in the Bible concerning the hidden manna, the budding rod, and the law of life because they lack experience. However, in the Lord's recovery, all these riches are being recovered among us.

When we partake of the hidden manna, we are not experiencing a Christ on the altar, nor are we partaking of a Christ on the showbread table. We are enjoying a Christ who is in the golden pot within the ark. Here we are beyond the world and every situation. We are beyond ourselves and our natural being, touching the divine nature and partaking of it. Second Peter 1:4 says, "Whereby are given unto us exceeding great and precious promises: that by these ye might be partakers of the divine nature." Unless we touch the golden pot, it will be difficult for us to partake of the divine nature. The divine nature is here with the golden pot in the ark. In the golden pot, that is, in the divine nature, there is the hidden manna as the special portion for our enjoyment. It is here that we enjoy the hidden Christ, the Christ who is hid in God with us and the Christ with whom we are hid in God. The Christ hidden in God is the manna hidden in the golden pot. Here Christ is the hidden manna, and here we also are hidden with Him in the divine nature.

If we are in the wilderness far off from the tabernacle, we can, by God's mercy, still enjoy the open manna as a normal experience in the wilderness. But this is too shallow, too outward, and too far off. God wants us to enter into the Holy of Holies and to be so intimate and close to Him, touching the golden pot. The hidden Christ as the heavenly hidden manna is here in God's divine nature. We cannot find Him in any other place. Today God's divine nature is in our spirit. Although we have the golden pot, the problem is that often we are far off from our spirit. You need not be quarreling or fighting with others in order to be out of the spirit. Even when you joke with the brothers you are outside the spirit. Also being religious is much different from being in the spirit. By being religious we are carried out to the wilderness. The golden pot is in the ark, and the ark is in the Holy of Holies, and the Holy of Holies is joined to our spirit. I like the hymn which says,

> In my spirit deeper still
> I would touch the Lord I love,
> Touch Him in His hidden depth
> And His hidden manna prove.

Within the Holy of Holies is the very Christ who is the ark of God containing the golden pot. This Christ comprises the divine nature and contains the hidden manna, for the hidden Christ is within the divine nature. In order to touch this special portion, this topmost portion, of Christ, we must touch the divine nature. In principle, everyone who enjoys this portion is in the Holy of Holies.

Everyone who enters into the Holy of Holies is with the High Priest. Christ, our High Priest, is in the Holy of Holies, and we also must be there. We must not only be the priests in the outer court or in the Holy Place; we must also be the priests where the golden pot is—in the Holy of Holies. If we would be in this place, we must be beyond the world and every kind of situation. We must be beyond being bothered by people. Sometimes we are offended by a small, unpleasant word. Some are troubled to such an extent that they cannot sleep well for months. If we are troubled in this way, we are far off from our spirit, and thus it will be difficult for us to be in the Holy of Holies. When we are beyond all situations, good or bad, pleasant or unpleasant, then we are in our spirit touching the ark and the golden pot. I say again that in this golden pot is the hidden manna, the hidden Christ, as our special portion. If we would partake of the hidden manna, we must constantly be in our spirit touching the divine nature. May we all go on and enter into this experience.

LIFE-STUDY OF HEBREWS

MESSAGE SIXTY

ENJOYING THE HIDDEN MANNA IN THE PRESENCE OF GOD

THE DISTANCE BETWEEN US AND THE LORD

In this message we need to consider some principles regarding spiritual food. The eating of spiritual food altogether depends upon the distance between us and the Lord. This distance determines how much spiritual food we can eat. If we are far off from the Lord, we cannot partake of any spiritual food. When the children of Israel were in Egypt, they could not eat the manna, because the manna was the spiritual food for God's people in the wilderness. Those who were in the wilderness were closer to God than those who were in Egypt. At that time, God was not in Egypt; He was in the wilderness. If anyone wanted to partake of spiritual food, the heavenly manna, he had to leave Egypt and go into the wilderness. As long as the Israelites were in Egypt, they had no spiritual food. Even if an Israelite was in the wilderness, he still had to be near the camp of the children of Israel in order to partake of the manna. If he was far away from the camp, it would have been difficult for him to enjoy the heavenly manna. Anyone who wanted to eat the manna had to camp with the children of Israel. By this we see that the distance between us and the Lord is a very important matter in the enjoyment of spiritual food.

The manna came down near the camp, and only those who had come out of Egypt and who were camping with God's people had the privilege of enjoying it. After the children of Israel had enjoyed the manna, God commanded the Israelites to present an omer of manna to Him (Exo. 16:33). The manna had come from God to them, and they offered a portion of it back to God. What is the hidden manna? The hidden manna is simply the top portion of the manna given by God and offered back to God. It is the special portion of manna. Once the manna had been presented to God, it was no longer the open manna; it had become the hidden manna because, after being presented to God, it was placed in a golden pot and hidden in the ark in the Holy of Holies within the tabernacle. Originally, the manna was under the sky in the open air. It was open to anything and anyone. But after the top portion had been presented to God and placed in the pot, it was hidden within the innermost part of the tabernacle, the Holy of Holies, where it was placed before the testimony of God. Among the children of Israel was the tabernacle, within the tabernacle was the Holy of Holies, within the Holy of Holies was the ark, within the ark was the golden pot, and within the pot was the manna. Hence, manna was altogether hidden. In this way, the top portion of manna became hidden.

Suppose you are an Israelite who has come out of Egypt and who is camping with God's people. You have the privilege of eating the open manna, but you do not have the right to enjoy the hidden manna. Because you are far off from the innermost chamber of the tabernacle, you do not have the right to enjoy the hidden manna. Where is God? He is in the Holy of Holies, in the innermost chamber of the tabernacle. Compared with the Egyptians and the others in the wilderness, you are closer to God. But, being outside the outer court of the tabernacle, you are not that close to Him. Although you may eventually come into the outer court, you still cannot enter into the Holy Place, much less into the Holy of Holies. If you are a priest, you may be in the Holy Place and be closer to God than the Levites who are serving in the outer court. Nevertheless, although you may be a priest ministering in the Holy Place, you are not yet in the Holy of Holies. Thus, there is still a distance between you and God. If you want to enjoy the hidden manna, there must be no distance between you and God. All the distance between you and the Lord must be eliminated.

In this message I do not care to explain what the hidden

manna is, for the more I explain it, the more troubled you will be. Rather, I would ask this question: how close are you to the Lord? Is there still a distance between you and Him? If there is, you may enjoy the open manna, but you cannot eat the hidden manna. If we would partake of the hidden manna, there must be no distance between us and the Lord. This matter of distance is quite exposing. Although we may not know what the hidden manna is, we do know how far we are from the Lord. Where are you? Are you in Egypt? Are you in the wilderness, or across the street from the tabernacle? Are you in the outer court, the Holy Place, or the Holy of Holies? If we are honest, some would say that they are in the outer court of the church life. Even in the church life there are sections: the section of the outer court, the section of the Holy Place, and the section of the Holy of Holies. Even in the Holy of Holies there are some small sections. If you are in the outer court or in the Holy Place of the church life, you cannot touch the hidden manna. You can only eat the sacrifices on the altar or the showbread on the table. You are still not in the place where the hidden manna is.

After the children of Israel had entered into the good land, they ate the produce of the land. In the Old Testament we are told clearly that all the children of Israel who were in the good land could partake of the produce of the land at any time. But anyone who was outside the border of the land had no right to enjoy this produce. Here again we see the matter of distance. When the children of Israel came together to eat at the time of the three yearly feasts, they did not eat the general produce, but the portion of the produce which was purposely reserved for the feast. At ordinary times, the Israelites enjoyed the common portion. At the time of the feasts, however, they enjoyed the special portion, the one top tenth, because they were closer to God, having come together to meet around God's dwelling place where they enjoyed the top portion of the produce of the good land, which they had offered to God (Deut. 12:17-18; 14:22-23). Another tenth of their produce was given to the priests and the Levites who served in the outer court or in the Holy Place and who were closer to God than most of the people were. Thus, the closer an Israelite was to God, the better was his enjoyment of the spiritual food. According to Numbers 18:26-28, after the priests and the Levites received the tithe, they offered one tenth of the tenth to the Lord. This topmost portion, which was offered to God as a heave offering, was then given to the high priest who ministered to God in the Holy of Holies. Since he was the one closest to God, he had the right to enjoy the topmost portion of the produce of the good land.

If we would be fed by God, we must be within the realm in which God feeds His people. Otherwise, we cannot enjoy any spiritual food. If we stay within this realm, we are privileged to enjoy spiritual food. However, if we remain close to the border of this realm, only the common part of the spiritual food will be ours. But if we come to the center, to God, we shall enjoy the better portion of this spiritual food. If I am an Israelite in the good land, I have the right to enjoy the common portion of the produce of the land. But if I seek God, going to the temple at the time of the yearly feasts, I shall be closer to the Lord and have the privilege of enjoying something better three times a year. This is not the common portion; it is a special portion of the produce of the land. If I am a Levite in the outer court or a priest in the Holy Place, I can enjoy a better portion of the produce of the land every day. If I am a high priest ministering in the presence of God, being so close to Him, I have the right to enjoy the best portion, the topmost portion, of the produce of the good land. Hence, the portion of the spiritual food which is ours depends upon the distance between us and the Lord.

THE HIDDEN MANNA PROMISED TO THE OVERCOMERS

Some may say that the hidden manna was kept only for a memorial, not for eating. If we did not have Revelation 2:17, this argument might have some meaning. But in this verse the Lord promises that the omer of manna which is kept in the presence of God as a memorial will be given to the overcomers to eat. It is not promised to the worldly

Christians, to those who are saved but who still remain in Egypt; neither is it promised to those who are wandering in the wilderness. It is a promise given to the overcomers in the church at Pergamos. The church at Pergamos was married to the world. It was a church that had gone back to Egypt, making God's house more worldly than the house of the Egyptians. The promise of eating the hidden manna was given to the overcomers who were in such a worldly church. This means that if we overcome being worldly, we shall be in the presence of God and have the privilege of eating the hidden manna. This manna has been hidden here for centuries. But now the Lord seems to be saying, "Because you hate the world, the worldly situation, the worldly church, and the worldly relationship between the church and the world, and because you are so close to Me, I will give you to eat of the hidden manna that has been kept in My presence." Before the Lord spoke this promise to the overcomers in Revelation 2:17, He said, "He that hath an ear, let him hear what the Spirit saith unto the churches." May we all have an ear to hear this.

For nearly twenty centuries, Christ has been given from the heavens as the open manna. But, under His economy, God has kept and is still keeping a special portion of Christ in His presence, and anyone who has a distance between himself and God has no right to eat it. Many Christians have enjoyed Christ as their open manna. If you read history and the biographies of the saints, you will see that many of them enjoyed Christ as the open manna. But the top portion of Christ has been kept in the presence of God and is here even now for those who refuse to go along with the church when it has become worldly and married to the world. In God's eyes, there has been a spiritual marriage between the degraded church and the world. Christ should be the church's husband. But today the church has married the world, not considering Christ to be her husband. For those dear ones who do not agree with this marriage but who stay strictly in the presence of God, the Lord has promised them the privilege of eating that portion of Christ which has been kept in the presence of God. This is the hidden manna.

MINISTERING TO THE LORD IN HIS PRESENCE

In the little booklet, "Ministry to the House or to the Lord," Brother Nee encourages us to minister to God, not to something good other than God. But look at the situation among Christians today. Nearly all Christians are ministering to something other than God, not to God Himself. They go to the mission field, preach the gospel, win souls, and teach the Bible. There are many such works, works which are for God, but which are other than God Himself. All those engaged in such work have the right to enjoy the open Christ, the open manna. But there is still the top portion of Christ which is kept in the presence of God, reserved especially for those who do not serve anything other than God Himself.

Today we are in the same situation as that of the church at Pergamos. Christianity has gone out from the presence of God. Not only apostate Christianity but even the so-called fundamental Christianity is far off from God's presence. Christianity does many things for God, but these things are not God Himself. Hence, there is a special portion of Christ kept in the presence of God for the dear ones who overcome the situation of the church in Pergamos. To overcome the condition of the church in Pergamos is to separate yourself from the general practice of today's Christianity and to remain in the presence of God ministering directly to Him, not to anything else. Here we have the enjoyment of the hidden manna, the special portion of Christ. Here we enjoy something of Christ which all those who are far off from His presence cannot taste.

Consider the service around the tabernacle in the Old Testament. The Levites served in the outer court, and the priests served in the outer court and in the Holy Place where they arranged the showbread, trimmed the lamp, and burned the incense. But when the high priest entered into the Holy of Holies, there was hardly any work to do. Here, in the Holy of Holies, the high priest ministered directly in the presence of God. Here, in the Holy of Holies, the ministering one enjoys the hidden manna. What is the hidden manna? It is that portion of Christ which we enjoy in the presence of God when there is no distance between us and Him.

As we all can testify, there have been many times when we realized that we were not very close to the Lord. Yet, although there was a distance between us and the Lord, we still enjoyed something of Him. Nevertheless, we had the sense that our enjoyment of the Lord was not that sweet. At other times we were somewhat closer to the Lord and sensed that our enjoyment of Him was sweeter. Some of the young people may still be tempted to go to the movies. If a young brother goes to a movie, he may, in a sense, still enjoy Christ while he is there. As he is watching the movie, Christ may disturb him, saying, "What are you doing here? Get out of here and don't come back anymore." What kind of experience is this? It is an experience of Christ as the most open portion of the open manna. Sometimes as Christian husbands and wives are exchanging words with one another, they have the sense, even as they are arguing, that they are enjoying Christ. When a brother is arguing with his wife, the Lord may say, "Stop! What are you doing here? You are just damaging the whole situation. Don't do this anymore. Go to your bedroom, kneel down, and pray to Me." This also is an enjoyment of Christ as the open manna. But at other times, when there is no distance between us and the Lord, we enjoy Christ in the most intimate and hidden way. This is the enjoyment of the hidden manna, the hidden portion of Christ.

Many of us who were involved in various types of Christian work in the past were enlightened to see that we could no longer participate in such work. We gave it up and took the narrow way. Outwardly, people said of us, "You are killing yourself." Yes, by giving up our work we were killing ourselves. But at the same time, after dropping our work for the Lord Himself, not allowing even the work of saving souls or of teaching the Bible to be a distance between us and the Lord, we immediately came into the direct presence of the Lord and enjoyed the hidden manna. Why can I not join so many types of work? Because such work is far from the presence of God. It is worldly, a sign of the church which has married the world and is full of worldliness. When we forsook that work, even at the cost of our lives, we were brought directly into the presence of the Lord. Many of us have had this experience.

In 1932 we began to have the church life in my home town. After approximately a year, the opposition came. I had been respected among the Christians, and nearly everyone loved me. But because of the church life, even some who were intimate with me would not greet me on the street. I was bothered by all the opposition and attack, thinking that I might be wrong in following the Lord in this way and wondering why the Lord's children were treating me so badly. However, as I went to the Lord regarding this, what intimacy there was between Him and me! I simply do not have the words to describe it. As I look back upon it now, I can see that it was the enjoyment of the hidden manna.

The hidden manna is the same as the open manna but in a different situation. When the manna is in the open air, it is the open manna. When it is in the presence of the Lord, concealed under several layers, it becomes the hidden manna. In nature, function, and every other aspect, the hidden manna is the same as the open manna. While there is no difference in nature or in function, there is a difference in position. The open manna is open to the public and the hidden manna is closed. We all must ask ourselves whether we would go along with worldly Christians or with God. If we go along with worldly Christianity, we may only enjoy the open manna, the open Christ. However, we shall be unable to enjoy the hidden Christ because He is always hidden in God.

The farther we are from God, the less service we have toward Him. The closer we are to Him, the more service we render to Him. Eventually, when we enter into the presence of the divine glory in the Holy of Holies, all service ceases. Here we only have the presence of the Lord and enjoy the hidden Christ, the hidden manna. It is here that we have direct fellowship with the Lord and know His heart and His intention. It is here that we can be charged with Him, with His intention, and with all He wants us to do. In this way we become a person who knows His heart and His intention. When we are such a person, His commitment will be ours. Why do we have God's commitment? Because we are in His presence. How do we know that we are in the presence of God? We know it from within and by realizing that there is no distance between us and God. We also know it by the deep inner sense that we are enjoying the hidden Christ as the top portion of the produce of the good land. This is the hidden manna. Praise the Lord!

LIFE-STUDY OF HEBREWS

MESSAGE SIXTY-ONE

THE BUDDING ROD

(1)

In this message we come to the matter of the budding rod (Heb. 9:4; Num. 17:1-10). Not many Christians have realized the full significance of the budding rod. Many simply regard the record of the budding rod as an interesting Bible story of a piece of dried wood that budded, blossomed, and yielded fruit overnight. But this incident is not a small point in the divine revelation.

Many Christians pay attention to the tabernacle. We have seen that with the tabernacle there are the altar and the laver in the outer court; the showbread table, the lampstand, and the incense altar in the Holy Place; and the ark of testimony in the Holy of Holies. The ark of testimony, the unique unit in the Holy of Holies, signifies Christ as the unique testimony of God. The contents of the ark comprise three items: the hidden manna, the budding rod, and the tables of the law. In the three previous messages, we have covered the first item, the hidden manna. Many Christians can understand something of the manna, for they know that it is a heavenly food signifying Christ as the bread of life. It is difficult, however, to understand the significance of the budding rod.

THREE SYMBOLS OF EXPERIENCES

The children of Israel had many experiences in the wilderness, and the Lord commanded them to place in His presence symbols of three of the experiences through which they passed. These symbols were the tables of testimony, the manna, and the budding rod. After the Israelites had received the law at Mount Sinai, the Lord told them to put the two tables of the law into the ark (Exo. 34:1, 29; 25:21; 40:20). An omer full of manna was put in a pot and laid up before the Lord to be kept (Exo. 16:32-34). In the wilderness, the children of Israel also passed through some experiences of rebellion. Numbers 16 is an account of the most serious rebellion. Out of that rebellion came the budding rod, which was put before the testimony, which was in the ark, as a sign (Num. 17:10-11). By this we see that each of these items came out of the experiences of the Israelites. They were not teachings, but the issue, the outcome, of their experiences. Thus, if we try to understand these three items by our mentality and for the purpose of acquiring knowledge, we shall not succeed. We can only understand them in, with, and for our experiences.

THE FOCUS OF THE DIVINE REVELATION

If we would understand the budding rod, we must have a little background. God's purpose is to gain a collective people to be His corporate expression to express and represent Him that He might have a dominion, a kingdom, in which to carry out His eternal economy. Many people think that God had a partial love for the Jews, working for them and doing things for them, and that He did not care for the Gentiles. This is a religious concept; it is not the focus of the divine revelation. The focus of the divine revelation is that the eternal God has a purpose. This purpose is to gain a people as a corporate unit to contain Him, to be one with Him, and to let Him be one with them that they might be the living expression of the invisible God, and that God might have a kingdom on earth to carry out His economy for His glory and to deal with His enemy. This was God's purpose when He called the children of Israel out of Egypt, making them a chosen and a called people.

THE NEED OF LEADERSHIP FOR THE BUILDING UP OF GOD'S PEOPLE

As such a people outside of Egypt, the Israelites were walking in the wilderness toward God's goal. The children of

Israel were at least a few million in number, for the male warriors alone numbered more than six hundred thousand (Num. 1:45-46). Since the number of the Israelites was so great, there was certainly the need, as there is today, for the building up of God's people. For the building up of the people of God, there was, in turn, the need for some authority. Using today's term, there was the need of leadership. As we shall see, God did not only raise up this leadership—He built it up. The leadership among the children of Israel was a corporate leadership comprising at least two men: Moses, representing the aspect of dominion and kingship, and Aaron, representing the aspect of image and priesthood.

THE PRIESTHOOD AND THE KINGSHIP

In order for God's people to express God and to represent Him, there must be both the priesthood and the kingship. Even the New Testament tells us clearly that in God's redemption He has made us priests and kings (Rev. 1:5-6; 5:9-10). Thus, we have the priesthood and we are in the kingship. We have the priesthood so that we may express God. This is related to the image of God. The kingship is for God's dominion. God created man in His image and gave him dominion over all the creatures (Gen. 1:26). This is the kingship for God's kingdom. In the church today there is still the need of the priesthood to express God and the kingship to represent God. In the coming millennial kingdom, we shall also be the priests expressing God and the kings representing God (Rev. 20:6). Furthermore, for eternity in the New Jerusalem we shall be priests and kings (Rev. 22:3-5) expressing God through our priesthood and representing Him with His dominion in our kingship. From the first chapter of Genesis through the last chapter of Revelation, the Bible is very consistent about these two aspects of God's corporate people.

THE BUILDING UP OF THE LEADERSHIP

Moses, representing the kingship, and Aaron, representing the priesthood, were put together for God's leadership. As we have already mentioned, they were both raised up and built up. God did not take Moses and put him into the leadership immediately after he had completed his education in Pharaoh's palace. No, after Moses had been educated, God brought him into the wilderness where He built up his leadership. Moses was born into a Jewish family and thus received the knowledge concerning God. Since he did not have a worldly education, God raised up the circumstances to enable him to receive the highest education in Pharaoh's palace (Acts 7:22). I believe that his education was higher than that of a Ph.D. Although he was so well educated, he was still not qualified to be the leader. During his first forty years, Moses learned of God and gained the world's best education. After that, he had to spend another forty years in the wilderness in order to be built up as a leader. The Bible does not afford us a clear record regarding the leadership of Aaron, but, in principle, Aaron must have also been under God's building hand. When Moses told the Lord that he was not eloquent but was "slow of speech, and of a slow tongue" (Exo. 4:10), the Lord said that Aaron, his brother, who could speak well, would be unto Moses "instead of a mouth" and that Moses would "be to him instead of God" (Exo. 4:14, 16). Only after Moses and Aaron had been built up as leaders were they able to take the lead.

THE REBELLION IN THE WILDERNESS

The journey through the wilderness was a test to the Israelites. When the Lord sent Moses to the children of Israel, He told him to speak to the people, saying on His behalf, "I will bring you up out of the affliction of Egypt unto...a land flowing with milk and honey" (Exo. 3:17). This was a good promise. The children of Israel were delivered out of the land of Egypt and they should have entered into the land of milk and honey. But due to their unbelief, which is recorded in Numbers 14, they could not enter in. Eventually, in Numbers 16, the rebels blamed Moses and Aaron, and not their own unbelief, for their not entering into the good land. The rebellious ones said, "Is it a small thing that thou has brought us up out of a land that floweth with milk and honey, to kill us in the wilderness, except thou make thyself altogether a prince over us? Moreover thou hast not brought us into a land that floweth with milk and honey" (Num. 16:13-14). Numbers 17:10 refers to these rebellious ones as "the rebels." The Hebrew word rendered rebels means "sons of rebellion." These sons of rebellion seemed to be saying to Moses and Aaron, "You promised to bring us into a land flowing with milk and honey, but you have not done it. Don't you know that the land out of which you brought us was a land of milk and honey? You have not fulfilled your promise." These sons of rebellion even said that Egypt was the land of milk and honey. What rebellion!

Who were these rebels? The first was Korah. Korah, who was a Levite (Num. 16:1), considered himself to be the same as Moses and Aaron, who also were Levites. Korah might have said within himself, "You two are Levites. How about me? Am I not also a Levite? Why must you take the lead, while I have no share in it?" Two of the other rebels were Dathan and Abiram, descendants of Reuben, the first son of Jacob. Considering themselves to be the tribe of the birthright, they might have said, "You Levites are number three, but we, the sons of Reuben, the first son of Jacob, are number one. Since you came after us, why should only the two of you take the lead?" Eventually, they all said to Moses and Aaron, "Ye take too much upon you, seeing all the congregation are holy, every one of them, and the Lord is among them: wherefore lift ye up yourselves above the congregation of the Lord?" (16:3). This was the subtle, devilish argument and condemnation within those rebels. What a rebellious root we see here!

NO LOSS OF TEMPER

Moses and Aaron were not young men. Both of them must have been about a hundred years of age. According to Psalm 90, which was written by Moses, the span of a human life is seventy years. If one's health is good, he might live to be eighty years of age. Hence, according to Moses' own writing, he should have been dead. But he was serving God after the age of death, and Aaron was even older than he. What was the good of their being so aged? The fact that it was not easy for them to lose their temper. The rebellion in Numbers 16 was serious and terrible, but it did not cause Moses to lose his temper. When the rebels gathered themselves together against Moses and Aaron, Moses "fell upon his face" (Num. 16:4). As we shall see in the next message, God came in to judge this rebellion.

THE VINDICATION OF THE PROPER LEADERSHIP

In Numbers 17 God seemed to be saying to Moses, "Those sons of rebellion were fighting with you over the leadership. Tell them that I shall do something to vindicate the leadership. I shall show them who the real leaders are, and their mouths will be shut." In Numbers 17:2 the Lord said to Moses, "Speak unto the children of Israel, and take of every one of them a rod according to the house of their fathers, of all their princes according to the house of their fathers twelve rods: write thou every man's name upon his rod." A rod is a piece of dead and dried-up wood. Its nature is that of dead wood. What is the function of a rod? It is to rule over others. A rod is different from a staff. A staff is for helping and supporting those who are weak and crippled and who have difficulty standing or walking. But a rod is not for supporting; it is for ruling and beating. According to the book of Proverbs, a father must use a rod to discipline his children (Prov. 23:13-14).

Our God is very wise, and He had the best way to vindicate the leadership. God did not argue. Rather, He seemed to say, "Since you have been arguing about the leadership, I ask you to bring your rods in before the testimony. You thought that you had the rods and could rule over others, and that Moses and Aaron assumed too much. You said that since you are all the people of God you all have the same authority. Do you have authority? Every tribe has a rod. Bring your rods to Me and put them in front of My testimony for a night, and let us see what will come out." In Numbers 17:5 the Lord said, "And it shall come to pass, that the man's rod, whom I shall choose, shall blossom: and I will make to cease from me the murmurings of the children of Israel, whereby they murmur against you."

Twelve rods were laid up before the Lord in the tabernacle of witness (Num. 17:7). Numbers 17:8 says, "It came to pass, that on the morrow Moses went into the tabernacle of witness; and, behold, the rod of Aaron for the house of Levi was budded, and brought forth buds, and bloomed blossoms, and yielded almonds." This signifies that the real leadership, the real authority, is in the budding life. This life not only buds and blossoms; it yields fruit that we might feed others, not that we might beat them. Although the rod is for ruling, this ruling is for feeding, not for beating.

The leadership among God's people is different from that found among the Gentiles. All the Gentile kings use their rods for ruling. No rod among the Gentile leaders is useful for feeding, because none of their rods is living. Every rod is just a piece of dead wood. Only with the proper leadership among God's people is there a rod budding with resurrection life and yielding fruit to nourish others.

The almond tree is the first tree in the year to blossom, blossoming in either January or February. The first fruit which comes out of a tree is the almond. This signifies resurrection. Hence, the budding, blossoming, fruit-yielding rod signifies the resurrection life of Christ. The leadership among God's children must be Christ Himself as the resurrection life which buds, blossoms, and bears almonds to feed God's people.

AMBITION FOR LEADERSHIP

Some may say, "I am not an elder and I don't want to be a leader among the Lord's children. I want to be free, take it easy, and not be bothered by this kind of thing." Although you may say this, I do not believe it, for everyone likes to be a leader. If you say that you do not like to be a leader, you are a liar. Deep within, you enjoy being a leader. When the service groups are arranged, you like to be number one. You do not want to be the last. The sisters may say, "As females, we don't care for the leadership." Sisters, do not say this. Suppose a piano service group is formed which includes five sisters. Every sister on the group will be concerned about the order in which the names are mentioned. When the fifth sister hears that her name is mentioned last, she may be so bothered that she will be unable to pray for a week. She may say, "If I can't be the first, I should at least be the third, but I'm not even the fourth. I have been saved for over fifteen years. Why should I be the last? What have the elders done? Don't they have any discernment?" This is the ambition for leadership.

I thank the Lord for this ambition. It is a good ambition, far better than the ambition to be the President of the United States. It is good that Christians have such ambition. If we had no ambition, we would be like chairs and benches, and God could do nothing with us. But because we are so ambitious, God can do something with us. Probably only those who are aged are no longer ambitious. A brother who is close to eighty years of age may have no ambition, but a young man may desire to be today's Apostle Paul. I encourage all the young people to be like this. I would be happy if all the young people would desire to be today's Peter or Paul.

In our life-study of Genesis, we have seen that Abraham, Isaac, and Jacob plus Joseph are aspects of one complete person in the experience of life. In like manner, we should not consider Korah as being separate from Moses. In our nature, we have the same ambition Moses had. When Moses was forty, he was ambitious to take the lead to rescue God's people from the tyranny of the Egyptian king (Acts 7:23-27). However, in Moses there was also the rebellious element of Korah, Dathan, and Abiram. Young brothers, I know that you have both the positive nature of Moses and the rebellious nature of Korah within you. Even worse, the negative elements of Dathan and Abiram are also in you. In the following message, we shall see that God has judged the rebellious nature and resurrected the positive element, the element of resurrection life.

If you had never been saved, you would have no ambition among God's people. Why are you so ambitious in the church life? Simply because you love the Lord. If you did not love the Lord and if you had no ambition, you would be like the street people, wandering about aimlessly, having no ambition to be anything for God. But today, as those who are in the church loving the Lord, you are ambitious and expect that one day you will be qualified for the leadership. This is a good ambition, yet it must be resurrected. But we must also realize that within us we also have Korah, Dathan, Abiram, and all the rebellious elements. At the same time that we are ambitious for God's goal, we are also rebellious. I understand this very well because I have been sick of this disease myself.

THE REBELLION OF THE SOUL AGAINST THE SPIRIT

Not only is there within us the rebellion against other leaders, but many times our soul rebels against our spirit. Often our mind says, "Spirit, why cannot I serve God? Why cannot I, the mind, do something for God?" Have you not had this kind of rebellion within you? Many times my soul has rebelled against my spirit, saying, "Spirit, I don't agree with this. I am smarter than you are and I can do a great deal. You are a part of Witness Lee. Am I, the soul, not also a part of Witness Lee? Are we not all the children of God? Why do you, the spirit, take so much upon you?" Many times in functioning we have used our soul in a rebellious way to show that our soul can do something for God and that we, the natural man, can do some service for God without exercising our spirit. This is a type of rebellion.

THE AMBITION AND REBELLION WITHIN US

Do not consider the children of Israel in Numbers 16 as being separate from one another. We must look at them as a collective person, a corporate person, who includes Moses, Aaron, Korah, Dathan, and Abiram. Within us, there are both Moses and Aaron and Korah, Dathan, and Abiram.

Both ambition and rebellion are in our being. Sometimes we cannot help laughing at ourselves, for we are so ambitious for God, yet we are so rebellious. I believe that everyone of us has experienced being ambitious and rebellious at the same time. Unless you have no heart for God, you have experienced this. As soon as you began to have a heart for God, you found that both ambition and rebellion were within you. The first rebellion is the rebellion of the soul, the mind, against your own spirit. The second rebellion is your rebellion against those who are over you or before you.

Although you may not admit it, this rebellion is in you. You may say, "Brother So-and-So, I love you and I submit myself to you." But while you are saying with your lips that you submit to Brother So-and-So, deep within you are rebellious, saying to yourself, "Brother So-and-So, you have taken too much upon you. You are altogether too much! In some aspects you are not as qualified as I am. One day my qualifications will be vindicated by God." This is the rebellion within you.

JUDGMENT AND VINDICATION

Thank God for ambition and, in a negative sense, thank God for rebellion. The rebellion in Numbers 16 brought in God's judgment and vindication. Firstly, God judged the rebels. After judging the rebellious element, the Lord commanded that the brass censers of the rebellious ones be made into plates for the covering of the altar as a sign to the children of Israel (Num. 16:36-40). After this, God told Moses to have twelve rods laid before His testimony. This was not for judgment; it was for vindication. Out of this vindication, the budding rod came forth. God then told Moses to bring Aaron's rod before the testimony "to be kept for a sign against the rebels" (Num. 17:10). Hence, there were two signs—the brass plates covering the altar, which came as a result of God's judgment, and the budding rod before the testimony, which came through God's vindication.

Ambition and rebellion are both within us. We all have

them, for we are the real Israel. Among and within the Israelites there were both ambition and rebellion. Firstly, God judged and burned the rebellious element. This judgment was then followed by God's vindication. As a result of this judgment and vindication, two signs came forth—one at the altar in the outer court and the other in the ark in the Holy of Holies. These signs indicate that our natural, rebellious nature must be judged and burned, and that resurrected ambition must be vindicated, and made to bud, blossom, and yield fruit. In this way we have the proper leadership.

In the ark in the Holy of Holies we experience Christ as the real leadership. Concerning the leadership, there are two aspects. The first is that the natural, rebellious element must be burned on the altar. The second is that in the Holy of Holies whatever has been regenerated into us and whatever belongs to the resurrected life must be enriched, strengthened, and made to bud, blossom, and bear almonds. Here is real leadership.

EVERY MEMBER, LIKE THE LEADER, BEING A SERVING ONE

A leader among the Lord's people is a serving one. Although you may not be an elder or the leader of a service group, you are still a serving one. In principle, you are the same as a leader in the Lord's service. Every member of the church is a serving one. God's building depends upon the serving ones. As a serving one, there is in you the rebellious element which must be judged and burned on the altar as a sign to the universe that your natural man has been dealt with. But there is also another element within you—the regenerated element, the life element which is Christ Himself as the resurrection life. When you get into the ark in the Holy of Holies and touch Christ as the resurrection life, this element will become your leadership. It will bud, blossom, and yield almonds for the nourishment of others.

Even the youngest brothers and sisters are serving ones. But their rebellious nature must also be burned, dealt with, and judged, and the resurrection life within them must bud, blossom, and yield almonds to feed others. Even within the youngest brothers and sisters are both ambition and rebellion. Even they have criticized the elders.

Praise the Lord for our proper ambition. Nevertheless, we must recognize that we also have the rebellious element. As long as these two things, the ambition and the rebellion, are fighting within us, the building can never go on. Thus, there is the need to judge the rebellion and to vindicate the ambition. The element of Christ within us must be vindicated, strengthened, enriched, uplifted, and made to bud, blossom, and yield almonds. The judgment is upon the rebellion, and the vindication is upon the ambition. We do have such a proper ambition. As we walk the path from the altar to the budding rod, the rebellion must be eliminated and the positive ambition must be released. Then we shall have the proper leadership and the proper service which are for the building up of God's people. God's building depends upon this budding rod, which can only be experienced within the ark in the Holy of Holies. For this, we must come forward to enter the Holy of Holies and enjoy the very Christ who is the unique ark of God's testimony.

LIFE-STUDY OF HEBREWS

MESSAGE SIXTY-TWO

THE BUDDING ROD

(2)

As we pointed out in the last message, few Christians have paid attention to the budding rod in Hebrews 9:4. The reason for this is that the budding rod is a matter of experience. Although we may understand the types of the tabernacle, we cannot know the true significance of the tabernacle until we have had the necessary experiences. As far as the experience of the tabernacle is concerned, the writings and messages of the various Christian teachers mainly speak of the altar. But once we go on from the altar to the Holy Place, we find that not many have touched the real experiences there. Thus, throughout the years, the three items in the ark in the Holy of Holies have remained a mystery. Few have even talked about them. Have you ever heard a message on the hidden manna, the budding rod, and the two tables of the law contained in the ark? This shortage is altogether due to the lack of experience.

THE BUDDING ROD AND THE BUILDING UP OF GOD'S PEOPLE

The budding rod is related to the building up of God's people. If we only had Hebrews 9:4, we could not see this. But if we consider the first mention of the budding rod in the Old Testament, we shall see that it is fully related to the building up of God's people. In the previous message we pointed out that for the fulfillment of His purpose God had to have a people as a corporate unit. In the Old Testament, this people was the children of Israel. They were at least a few million in number and had to be built up as one.

According to the record of the history of Israel, they were treated as one unit. The Bible does not say that they were saved individually. No, they were all saved corporately. They held the Passover all together as a corporate people and they all crossed the Red Sea as one unit. Moses did not cross the Red Sea alone, with Aaron following him a few days later. Even as they were wandering in the wilderness, they were a corporate people, not a group of individuals with everyone taking his own way. Moreover, among them was the tabernacle, God's unique dwelling place. There was not one tabernacle of God in Moses' backyard and another one in Aaron's yard. There was just one tabernacle which, as God's unique dwelling place, was the center for the building up of God's people. As we have seen, in order for so many to be built up together, there was the need of the leadership. The budding rod is related to this leadership and is for the building up of God's people.

Korah, who belonged to the tribe of Levi, the same tribe to which Moses and Aaron belonged, considered himself to be equal to Moses and Aaron. Korah might have said, "Moses and Aaron, you are children of Levi. I am, too. I am the same as you are." Along with Korah, there were Dathan and Abiram, descendants of Reuben, the first son of Jacob. Dathan and Abiram probably thought that because their tribe was the first, they also should be among the leaders. These three men stirred up a great rebellion. According to Numbers 16:2, Korah, Dathan, and Abiram "rose up before Moses, with certain of the children of Israel, two hundred and fifty princes of the assembly, famous in the congregation, men of renown." As Numbers 16 indicates, nearly the whole congregation of Israel rebelled against Moses and Aaron. Undoubtedly, that rebellion was the work of the enemy to destroy the building among God's people. It surely hindered the children of Israel from going on to reach God's goal. I mention this to show that the budding rod is related to the building up of God's people.

When many Christians read Hebrews 9, they pay no attention to the budding rod because among them there is not the building up of God's people. I would like to address a question to those who have been Christians for many years: have you ever heard a message telling you that what God needs today is the building up of His people? There is no such thing in today's Christianity. Because most Christians do not pay attention to this matter of the building, they are not interested in the budding rod. Many today talk about spirituality, gifts, behavior, and speaking in tongues, but who is concerned about the building up of God's people? Without the building up of His people, there is no way for God to fulfill His purpose. God wants a people that is built up as a unique unit. As the Head, Christ needs the Body, not many separate members. And God needs a house, not a pile of stones. This is what God is after today. If we are not for this, we have neither the standing nor the qualifications to understand the significance of the budding rod. If you have no interest in God's eternal purpose but are still for the world, everything in this message will merely be vain talk as far as you are concerned.

May the Lord be merciful to us that we may see that what He is seeking today is the building. It is not a question of how spiritual we are, nor how good we are, nor how gifted we are; it is a question of whether or not we have been truly built up with God's people. Today there is too much religion, too much of the human concept, and too little divine revelation. If we would understand the significance of the budding rod, we must have a heavenly, divine vision that God's need today is for the building up of His people. What matters to God is not how many people He has, but whether or not they have been built up. If we are here for God's eternal purpose, then we must see that God's need is for the building.

Consider the tabernacle. There is no building at the altar. What we see at the altar is the sacrifice for redemption. Although this is wonderful, it is not God's goal. It is the beginning, not the end. As we have seen already, the experience of the tabernacle starts with the altar and consummates with the ark. Within the ark there are three items—the hidden manna, the budding rod, and the tables of the law. At the altar we see nothing regarding the building. Neither do we have the building at the laver. The washing of the life-giving Spirit at the laver is for the building, but it is not the building itself.

From the laver we proceed to the showbread table, where there is much food for us to eat. But eating should not simply be for eating; it also must be for the building. The term hidden manna is used only once in the New Testament. It is found in Revelation 2:17 which says, "To him that overcometh will I give to eat of the hidden manna, and will give him a white stone." This verse indicates that eating the hidden manna transforms us into a white stone. Eating the hidden manna transforms us into an acceptable stone, and this transformation is for God's building. Eventually, as Revelation 3:12 indicates, the eating ones are built into God's temple. By this we see that eating is for the building. At the showbread table, however, we still do not see the building. Hence, we must not stop here but continue on to our destination.

From the showbread table we go to the lampstand and from there to the incense altar. At neither of these two stations do we see the building. Then we enter into the Holy of Holies, touch the ark, and find within it the budding rod. Why was the budding rod not found at the altar? If it were at the altar, you could never have any experience of the ark. If you enter into the Holy of Holies and experience the ark, you will discover that in the ark is a basic item—the budding rod. Following this, we must learn the significance of the budding rod—that it is related to God's building. If you are seeking the Lord, you must realize that God's goal is to bring you to the budding rod within the ark in the Holy of Holies.

As we have seen, the budding rod signifies that Christ, the resurrected One, should be our life, our living, and the resurrection life within us, and that this life should bud, blossom, and bear almonds. Is the Christ within you budding? Do not say yes doctrinally, but answer according to your experience. Is your Christ budding, blossoming, and bearing almonds, the fruit of resurrection?

THE AMBITION FOR POSITION

Recently, a brother gave a testimony about being assigned to a service group. When he heard that he had been put on that service group, he wondered whether his position in that group would be the first or last. When he learned that he was not number one, he was somewhat disappointed. That testimony revealed to me that even among us there is the ambition for position. Everyone likes to be number one. Not only is there the ambition for position among us, but also the ambition for promotion. In the church service, the second one is endeavoring to be promoted to the position of number one. Furthermore, those who are first are afraid of losing their leading position. When I learned of this, something within me said, "Do you believe that all the saints in the Lord's recovery are so spiritual that they don't care for position or promotion? Do you think that they just love the Lord and have no ambition for anything? You are too spiritual. There is not such a spiritual condition here." The ambition for position and promotion is found among us.

GOD'S JUDGMENT ON REBELLION

Being ambitious, however, does not work, except in the negative sense of working out God's judgment upon us. In the last message we pointed out that we should not consider Moses, Korah, Dathan, and Abiram as separate individuals but as parts of a corporate people. Likewise, you should not consider yourself only to be like Moses. Although I do not know whether or not you are Moses, I am quite sure that Korah, Dathan, and Abiram are within you. We all have these rebellious elements within us, for we were born with them. We all were born Korahs. But by God's mercy and grace, the real Moses element is being wrought into us. Without His mercy and grace, we would only be Korah. If in Numbers 16 Korah, Dathan, and Abiram had been dormant, probably nothing would have happened. But they were very ambitious and seemed to say, "Moses and Aaron, are you the only leaders? Are we not leaders also?" Because of this, God's judgment was brought in. The earth swallowed up

Korah, Dathan, and Abiram (Num. 16:31-33), and "there came out a fire from the Lord, and consumed the two hundred and fifty men that offered incense" (Num. 16:35).

TWO SIGNS

After this judgment upon rebellion, God commanded that the brass censers of the two hundred and fifty men who were consumed by fire be made into plates for the covering of the altar as a "sign unto the children of Israel" (Num. 16:36-40). These brass plates on the altar became a sign of God's judgment on rebellion. In this we see that the altar is not only a place for our redemption but also a place for our judgment. At the altar the natural element in us is judged, and that judgment remains as a sign, a memorial, and an indicator that our natural life and our natural element must be judged and burned.

In Numbers 16 and 17 there are two signs, one at the altar and the other in the ark. The sign at the altar is the judgment of the natural element (Num. 16:38), and the sign in the ark is the resurrection of the resurrected life (Num. 17:10). In Numbers 17 God told Moses to bring twelve dead rods, one for each of the twelve tribes, and to place them in His presence for a night. That each rod was a dead stick signified that the leaders of the twelve tribes were nothing but dead wood. The next morning one of the twelve rods budded, blossomed, and yielded almonds. This rod did not live by itself but by the resurrection life. This indicated that firstly our natural element must be judged and burned. Our ambition for position and promotion must be burned. Whenever we come into the tabernacle, we must firstly come to the altar and see there a sign of God's judgment upon our natural element. Both our sin and our natural element must be judged at the altar of brass. After experiencing this judgment at the altar, we may proceed to the laver, the showbread table, the lampstand, the incense altar, and then come forward to the ark in the Holy of Holies. Here in the ark we can see the budding rod. This is the second sign.

The first sign, the brass plates on the altar, signifies that our natural element must be judged and burned. This negative element has no share in God's building. In God's building there is no room for anything natural. If you want to participate in the leadership, your natural Korah, Dathan, and Abiram must be judged and burned, and that judgment must remain as a reminder to you. Whenever you come into God's service, you then will see that reminder on the altar. If we would participate in God's service, we must realize that our natural element must be judged. Whether you desire to be the first or the last, you still must be judged and burned on the altar. The first thing in God's building is His judgment.

Although you may love the Lord and care for His testimony, within you there are the elements of Korah, Dathan, and Abiram. At times, the Lord may say to you, "This natural element must be judged. You love Me and you care for My testimony—that is wonderful. But your natural element must be dealt with and condemned." If this does not happen every month, it may happen at least every six months. The more you experience this, the brighter will shine the brass on the altar as a reminder that your natural man must be judged. Hallelujah, for these two signs! One sign is at the altar, and the other is in the ark. In the ark is the budding rod signifying the resurrected Christ in our spirit. This budding rod is the authority.

Suppose that two ambitious brothers are struggling against one another for the leadership, and that only one of them has passed through the experience of Numbers 16 and has been judged and dealt with. The brass on the altar reminds him of God's judgment upon him. As the issue of this experience, he has the budding rod. In a very real sense, the budding rod comes out of the brass altar. In like manner, the resurrection life comes out of the judgment of God upon our natural life. The brother who is struggling against him, however, has not had his natural man dealt with. The brother who has experienced both the judgment of the altar and the budding rod in the ark may be small and rather unintelligent, and the brother who has not been dealt with may say, "Am I not more capable than he? Surely I am. But whatever I do results in death. It is the issue of a rod of dead wood. I'm just a dead stick, but this brother who is less skillful and intelligent than I am, buds, blossoms, and bears almonds." If you bring a case to the natural brother, the issue will always be death, for he is a dead rod and can do nothing but kill. But if you bring a case to the brother with the budding rod, the issue will be buds, blossoms, and fruit. If a deadened person stays with him for a while, he will become alive. As a result, the natural brother will say, "I can't understand why everything that comes to me in the church life becomes dead and everything that comes to this brother becomes so living. God is not fair." But God is more than fair.

NO COMPETITION IN THE CHURCH SERVICE

There should be no competition in the church service. Competition never works. The more you compete to be the first, the less you are qualified even to be the last. The more you compete, the more you will remain in your dead condition. It is not a matter of competition; it is a matter of being judged and of having the self, the natural life, and the natural element burned. Then at the altar there will be a reminder that our natural life must be dealt with and eliminated. Hundreds of us can testify that whenever we competed with others, we were killed. Whenever we say, "Why does God use him and not me?" we are finished. The more you say this, the less God will use you. The more competitive you are, the less qualified you will be. During the past years I have not seen an exception to this among the Lord's children. We all need to say, "There's nothing good in me. I'm filled with Korah, Dathan, Abiram, and with so many natural things that must be judged on the brass altar." Whoever is willing to be judged will immediately be brought into the Holy of Holies and have the budding rod, the resurrection life. When you are such a person, whatever comes to you, even if it is a dead situation, will issue in life.

THE BUDDING ROD BEING GOD'S VINDICATION

Many Christian organizations are unhappy with us. They say, "How can you claim to be the church? Are we not the church also?" Being the church is not a matter of what we say; it is a question of where the budding rod is. Whether people appreciate us or oppose us means nothing. The only thing that counts is the budding rod. If this is the church in Anaheim, the Lord's testimony in Orange County, it will bud, blossom, and yield almonds to nourish others with resurrection life. Whenever some rumors are spread about us or some papers are written against us, I tell the brothers that those rumors and papers mean nothing and that we should forget about them. The only thing that matters is whether or not we have the budding rod. The budding rod is God's vindication. Of the twelve rods laid up before the Lord, only one budded, blossomed, and yielded almonds. What will you say about this? Although Aaron's rod budded, the rebellious ones were still not convinced. They continued to murmur. Do not think that when the budding rod appears everyone in Orange County will be convinced. No, the more our rod buds, the more murmuring there will be.

What we need, and what the church needs, is the budding rod. Competition, promotion, position, and ambition mean nothing. From now on, in the church service there will be no number one, number two, nor any other number. Everyone is number nothing. We have no number because we are nothing; we are nobody. We all must be judged, and then we all must have the budding rod.

Having authority is not a matter of what we can do; it is a matter of how much we bud. You may do a great deal, but there is no blossoming. Instead of budding, you die; instead of blossoming, you kill others; and instead of bearing fruit, you deaden everyone who contacts you. This proves that you do not have the authority. However, if you have the budding rod and a dead one contacts you, he will be revived and become living. This proves that you have the authority. The authority is not in our capability or skill. The real vindication is in our budding, not in our doing. Doing means nothing, but budding means everything. In our church life and in the church service, we all must bud, blossom, and yield almonds. This is our need today.

THE WAY TO HAVE THE BUDDING ROD

Now we come to a very crucial point—the way to have the budding rod. The budding rod follows the hidden manna. This means that if we enjoy the hidden manna, we shall bud, for the issue of enjoying the hidden manna is the budding rod. How much you will bud with life depends on how much you eat of the hidden manna. We all need to exercise our spirit to contact the hidden Christ and to enjoy the topmost portion of the Christ hidden in the divine nature. The more we enjoy the hidden Christ as the highest portion in the divine nature, the more our rod will bud. There is no need for you to compete for any position, nor to care for anything. Simply enjoy the hidden manna which will nourish you and cause you to bud. As long as you are budding, you are the authority. If you bud, blossom, and yield almonds, others will know that you are the authority.

The authority among God's people today is neither capability nor position; it is the budding, the blossoming, and the fruit-bearing. We need to forget our past concern with competition, position, and promotion and have a new start. Among us in the Lord's recovery, we should not be concerned about position. We should only care for the enjoyment of the top portion of the hidden Christ, that we might be able to bud even during the dark night. Although the night is dark, we are budding, blossoming, and yielding almonds to nourish others. The one who buds, blossoms, and yields almonds is surely the authority among God's people.

In the book of Hebrews, we see that we must experience Christ at the altar, at the laver, at the showbread table, at the lampstand, at the incense altar, and at the ark in the

Holy of Holies. Here in the Holy of Holies we enjoy Christ in God's presence. This enjoyment causes us to bud, not with our ability but with the resurrected life. In this way, God can exercise His authority for the building up of His people. I have the full assurance that this is exactly what God is doing among us. He is causing us all to realize the judgment of the natural element and to participate in the resurrected life that we may bud, blossom, and yield almonds.

LIFE-STUDY OF HEBREWS

MESSAGE SIXTY-THREE

THE LAW—THE TESTIMONY OF GOD

As we have pointed out, in the ark in the Holy of Holies there were three crucial items: the hidden manna, the budding rod, and the tables of the law (9:4). In the past five messages we have somewhat covered the hidden manna and the budding rod. In this message we come to the tables of the law.

THE LAW BEING GOD'S TESTIMONY

In the Bible it is difficult to find the term the tables of the law. The Old Testament frequently speaks of the tables of the testimony (Exo. 31:18), and the New Testament mentions the tables of the covenant (Heb. 9:4). Why was the law called the tables of the testimony and the tables of the covenant? It is quite easy to understand why the law was called the tables of the covenant because in the Old Testament the law was the old covenant. It is difficult, however, to understand why the law was called the tables of the testimony. When God commanded Moses to build the ark (Exo. 25:10), He said, "Thou shalt put into the ark the testimony which I shall give thee" (Exo. 25:16). The testimony in this verse undoubtedly denotes the law. God did not say to put the law in the ark; He said to put the testimony into it. Because the testimony was placed in the ark, the ark was called the ark of the testimony (Exo. 25:22). Furthermore, the tabernacle was called the tabernacle of the testimony (Num. 17:8, Heb.). Hence, we have the testimony, the ark of the testimony, and the tabernacle of the testimony. When the manna and the budding rod were placed before the law, they were put in front of the testimony (Exo. 16:34; Num. 17:10). Whatever was placed in front of the testimony was before God

(Exo. 16:33-34), for the testimony could not be separated from Him. When something was before the testimony, it was before God, and when it was before God, it was before the testimony. What is this testimony? We have seen that the ark is called the ark of the testimony and that the tabernacle is called the tabernacle of the testimony. The law was called the testimony because it testified of God. For this reason, it was God's testimony.

In Genesis 1:26 we are told that God created man in His own image. God's intention is to have an expression through man. This expression is His testimony. Therefore, the testimony of God is the expression of God. It is God expressed. God's intention has been, still is, and for eternity will be the same—to work Himself into man that He may be expressed and have a testimony. But before God accomplished this, man fell. In his fallen nature, man tried to do good in order to please God. Because of this, God gave man the law. God gave man the law because man did not know that, as a fallen being, he could neither satisfy God nor express Him. After the law was given, however, God immediately changed the term, calling it the testimony. What God gave man was the law, but it was not mainly called the law but the testimony. In Psalm 119 the word testimony is used many times to denote the law (vv. 2, 88, 168). Every time this word is used in Psalm 119 it refers to the law.

According to man's concept, the law means the ten commandments. But God's intention was not that the law should be some commandments, but that it should be His testimony. When I was in Christianity, I never heard the term testimony used with respect to the law. I only heard about the ten commandments. In Christianity, when many young people are examined for membership in the so-called churches, they must recite the ten commandments. Although you may be able to recite the commandments, perhaps you have never heard that the testimony in Psalm 119 is the law. In fact, in the book of the Psalms the word testimony refers to the law. I say once again that in God's intention and according to His concept, the law is His testimony. But in the human concept, the law is the ten commandments. If you are trying to keep God's law, it will certainly be the ten commandments to you. But if you know what life is, and if, instead of trying to keep the law, you walk with God, you will realize that the law is God's testimony, God's expression.

THE TWO ASPECTS OF EVERY LAW

Every law has two aspects, the aspect of the law-keeper and the aspect of the law-maker. Laws are for people to keep. As we have mentioned several times in the past, the kind of law you make reveals the kind of person you are. If bank robbers could make laws, they would legalize bank robbing. Some legislators want to legalize such an evil thing as prostitution. This reveals that they themselves are evil. Evil lawmakers will enact evil laws. That the laws we make express the kind of people we are is true not only in a nation but also in a family. If the parents in a family get up very late every day and do not clean the house, they will make family laws which allow their children to get up late and to be messy. But if the parents are strict, clean, neat, and diligent, they will have a different family law. They will require their children to arise early in the morning, to wash themselves, and then to clean their rooms. If I visit this kind of home and see this type of regulation, I shall immediately know that the parents there must be diligent and clean. But if I go into a home where everything is a mess and where the children are allowed to sleep until late in the morning, I shall also realize what kind of people the parents in that home are. Since the laws we make testify to what we are, our law becomes our testimony. On the side of the law-maker, the law is a testimony; on the side of the law-keeper, the law is a commandment or regulation. God's law also has these two aspects. To us who attempt to keep the law, it is the ten commandments, but to God, it is His testimony.

THE LAW AS A TYPE OF CHRIST

I have read some books which say that the law is a type of

Christ. For a long time, I was troubled by this. How can the law, whose position is that of the concubine (Gal. 4:24), be a type of Christ? From the aspect of the law as commandments for us to keep, its position is that of the concubine. But from the aspect of the law as the testimony of God, it is a type of Christ. The real, living, full, and adequate testimony of God is just Christ Himself. Thus, the law typifies Christ as God's living testimony. Christ expresses God. The law was given, but Christ came to be the living expression of God (John 1:17). In the beginning was the Word, and the Word was God (John 1:1). Then the Word became flesh, full of grace and reality (John 1:14), for the purpose of being the expression of God. Because God is embodied in Christ, Christ is the living, full, and adequate testimony of God.

We have seen that the law is God's testimony, God's expression. If you want to know what kind of God God is, you should read the laws He has made. If you read the ten commandments, you will see that the Maker of those laws certainly must be a holy One, a righteous One, a loving One, One who is in the light. The ten commandments prove that God is holy and righteous and that He is love and light. God is a God of light and a God of love. He Himself is light and is love (1 John 1:5; 4:8), and He is holy and righteous. The law testifies that He is such a God. But the law was merely a testimony in letters. When Christ came, the testimony of God became living. It was no longer letters, but a living Person. While Jesus was on earth, He was God's living testimony. Wherever He went, He expressed God. Whatever He did, said, and thought expressed God. Because He was the embodiment of God, He was the expression and testimony of God. If in the days of the Old Testament you wanted to know what God was like, you had to consult the law. But today if you want to know what God is like, you must come to Jesus Christ. In the Old Testament the law was God's testimony, but today Jesus Christ is His living, full, and adequate testimony.

THE ULTIMATE AND CENTRAL ITEM IN THE TABERNACLE

Holding this concept of the law as the testimony of God will help us to understand Hebrews 9. Hebrews 9:4 mentions the tables of the covenant, referring to the tables of the testimony of the law. According to Hebrews 9, the tables of the covenant were the last of the items related to the tabernacle. In the outer court were the altar and the laver; in the Holy Place were the showbread table, the lampstand, and the incense altar; and in the Holy of Holies was the ark in which were the hidden manna, the budding rod, and the tables of the covenant. In this we see that the last and ultimate item is the tables of the covenant, that is, the testimony. The three items in the ark are deeper than those in the Holy Place. The items in the Holy Place are merely the beginning, but the items in the ark are the ultimate consummation. The ultimate consummation of the showbread is the hidden manna, the ultimate consummation of the incense altar is the budding rod, and the ultimate consummation of the lampstand is the testimony. Of all the things related to the tabernacle, the tables of the testimony are the topmost. Not only are they the top item; they are also the most central item. They are in the very center of the tabernacle.

In the tabernacle we can see a number of layers. The first layer is the curtain separating the tabernacle and the outer court from everything else, the second is the wall of the tabernacle, and the third is the veil separating the Holy of Holies from the Holy Place. The ark of the testimony, within which is the testimony, is the fourth layer. Thus, the testimony is in the center of the tabernacle.

THE LAW OF LIFE BEING IN CHRIST

As saved people, we are the temple of God (1 Cor. 3:16). Our body is the outer court, our soul is the Holy Place, and our spirit is the Holy of Holies. The law of life is neither in the outer court nor in the Holy Place but in the Holy of Holies. However, it is not sufficient to say that it is only in the Holy of Holies, for it is in the ark, that is, within the fourth layer. The law of life is in the ark, the ark is in the Holy of Holies, the Holy of Holies is in the tabernacle, and the tabernacle is within the separating curtain of the outer court. We have seen that the outer court is our body, that the Holy Place is our soul, and that the Holy of Holies is our spirit. What then is the ark? It is Christ. Since Christ is the ark, we should not say that the law of life is directly in our spirit. Although we have a spirit, if we do not have Christ in it, the law of life is not in our spirit. The law of life is in our spirit because the law of life is in Christ and Christ is in our spirit.

Why did God not tell His people to put the law in the altar? Why did He command them to put it into the ark? It would have been a mistake for God to put the law in the altar, because His intention was not that man should keep the law. No, according to God's concept, the law was to be His testimony. Therefore, He put His law in the ark in the Holy of Holies.

Do you think that you can be like God? It is impossible. If you read the ten commandments every day, prayed about them, fasted concerning them, and tried your best to keep them, you would still be unable to fulfill them. You can never make yourself correspond to God's law. Neither can you express Him. God's intention is not that we try to obey the law nor attempt to express Him. Firstly, His intention is to show us what He is. However greatly we may love the law, we cannot fulfill it. What then should God do? He said, "This is the covenant which I will covenant with the house of Israel after those days, says the Lord: I will impart My laws into their mind, and on their hearts I will inscribe them, and I will be God to them, and they shall be a people to Me" (8:10). God's intention is to put His law into us, into our inward parts and even into our heart. This does not mean that we should keep the law. No, it means that the law will work itself out from within us. This reveals why God put the law into the ark and put the ark into the Holy of Holies. How can this law get into us? Only through Christ.

When Christ gets into us, this law comes into us. When we received Christ, we received the law. The law is in Christ, and Christ is in our spirit. Thus, Romans 8:2 speaks of "the law of the Spirit of life in Christ Jesus." Not only is this law in Christ; it is Christ. When you received Christ and accepted Him as your Savior, you received the law of life.

LETTING CHRIST LIVE OUT OF US

When God gave the law to Moses, He did not intend that His people should keep it. He gave them the law to show them what kind of God He is and to reveal to them what He wants. Because He wants man to be His expression, He wanted them to be like Him, to be the same as He is. Although God had this desire, nothing happened. Instead, man tried to imitate God, attempting to make himself the same as God. But man failed. One day the real law, the living law, Christ, the reality of God's testimony, came, and we received Him into us. As a result, this real law, the reality of the law, has been wrought into the very center of our being. Now in the innermost part of our being is something wonderful—Christ Himself as the reality of the law. We have seen that the innermost matter in the tabernacle is the law. Today, the innermost thing within us is Christ in our spirit as the reality of the law. Now that we have this law within us, it is no longer a matter of our keeping the law; it is absolutely a matter of allowing Christ to live out of us. We should not try to keep the law from without, but let Christ live Himself out from within.

Every religion, whether it is Judaism, Catholicism, or Protestantism, is the same. God's intention is to put the law into our innermost part and to have us submit ourselves to it, not to try to keep it. Although we cannot keep the law, we should submit to it and let it live itself out of us. Religion, which teaches people to keep the law, is the exact opposite of this. When Christians read the Bible, they often select verses to keep as commandments. For example, the married brothers who are not good husbands always choose the commandment which says that the wives should submit to their husbands. But the better husbands choose the commandment which says that the husbands should love their wives. These brothers say, "O Lord, I can't fulfill this commandment. Please come in to help me. Lord, in the past I have not behaved as a loving husband. Forgive me and make me the best husband." Although you may pray in this way, you will never succeed. Such a husband must realize that the real love for his wife is Christ. Since this love is in us, we need not try to love. We should simply submit to this love, that is, to Christ, and let Him come out of us.

Take the example of humility. James 4:6 says, "God resisteth the proud, but giveth grace unto the humble." After reading this verse in the past, I prayed, "Lord, I want to be humble. But You know, Lord, that it's difficult for me to be humble. I ask You to please help me." This prayer is in the darkness of religion. One day, the Lord opened my eyes, and I saw that my name is pride and that I could never be humble. How can pride be humble? I am a dog. How can a dog be a bird? It is impossible. Our eyes must be opened to see that we can never be humble and that real humility is Christ. We should simply submit ourselves to Him and say, "Lord, You do it. It is no longer I, but Christ who lives in and out of me." If you simply submit to Christ, He will live Himself out of you, and you will become the expression and testimony of God. This is God's economy.

THE WAY TO HAVE CHRIST AS THE REALITY OF THE LAW

How can Christ as the reality of the law be real to us? Consider the contents of the ark once again. The first item, the manna, is firstly followed by the budding rod and then by the testimony. This implies and even indicates that when we eat and enjoy Christ as the hidden manna, something will bud in us. The manna we eat eventually becomes the budding element in us. The more we eat and enjoy Christ, the more He becomes our budding element. When this element blossoms and yields fruit, that is the testimony, the expression. Sometimes in the late afternoon I am exhausted and my stomach is empty. This indicates that I need to eat something. After I eat, I am filled and experience a quick transformation, for what I have eaten for dinner begins to blossom out of me, becoming my expression and testimony. In like manner, if we would experience Christ as the reality of the law, we must firstly eat the hidden manna. Once this manna gets into us, it will become the budding element, and this budding element will bring forth the fruit which is God's expression and testimony.

We should not stay at the altar, nor linger at the laver, nor even remain in the Holy Place eating the superficial food. We must come forward to the Holy of Holies, dive into the ark, and eat the hidden manna, the hidden Christ. This Christ will then become our budding element. When He buds and blossoms, He will yield the fruit which will be God's expression and testimony. This expression will correspond to and even surpass the ten commandments. Praise the Lord that now we are not in the outer court, nor even in the Holy Place, but in the Holy of Holies. Now that we are touching the ark and eating the hidden manna, we shall surely bud, blossom, and bear fruit. In this way, we shall have the testimony of God.

LIFE-STUDY OF HEBREWS

MESSAGE SIXTY-FOUR

THE LAW OF LIFE SPREADING IN OUR INWARD PARTS

THE BASIC CONCEPT OF THE DIVINE REVELATION IN THE BIBLE

If we would thoroughly understand and apprehend the law of life, we must understand the basic concept of the divine revelation in the Bible. The basic and central concept in the Bible is that God intends to work Himself into us in order to make us His living expression. God desires to work Himself into His chosen people that they may be born of Him and have Him as their life and thus become His expression. This is God's desire and intention. The only way for God to have such a living expression is for Him to work Himself into us. Although this basic concept is found throughout the Bible, it has nearly been lost by fundamental Christianity. Fundamental Christianity mainly stresses redemption. But redemption is not the goal; it is a way, a procedure, to reach the goal. The goal is to have God wrought into our being that we might be born of Him and that He might become our life. He is our Father and we are His sons. Being His sons, we all have Him in us as our life. Eventually, this life will transform us and conform us to His very image, making us His living expression in the universe.

Although this basic concept has nearly been lost, we thank God that now, in these last days, He has opened up to us this matter in His Word. For more than forty years, we have been burdened to minister this basic concept to God's people. It is for this reason that we have been falsely accused of teaching heresy, of preaching and teaching something that is not according to the Bible. Our opposers say this because their understanding of the Bible is lacking and inadequate. A little knowledge is dangerous, for it makes people short-sighted and even kills them. We praise God that under His mercy we have seen the basic revelation in the Scriptures. This is not simply a matter of redemption. No, it is something deeper and higher than this. God is now working Himself into us that we may have His life, that we may be one with Him, and that He may be one with us.

THE SON OF GOD COMING INTO US AS LIFE

I say again that the way in which God accomplishes His intention is by coming into us, causing us to be born of Him. In order that we might be born of Him, God comes into us in the Son, Jesus Christ. Jesus Christ, who is the Son of God and God Himself, is God's image. Colossians 1:15 says that Christ is the image of the invisible God. The Son is the image, the expression, of the Father. Thus, when you see the Son, you see the Father. At the moment we believed in Him, the Son of God came into us. This does not mean that He gave us something; it means that He Himself came into us. We need to discard the concept that when we believed in the Lord Jesus Christ, God gave us His life. This understanding is incorrect. It was not that we believed in the Lord Jesus and that God in heaven gave us something and put it into us. No, it was that we believed in the Lord Jesus and that the Son of God, the very God Himself, came into us as life. God did not give us His life; He came into us as life. What a great difference!

When God comes into us, He comes in the Son and as the Son, not as the Father. This involves the Trinity. It is at this point that we are accused of teaching heresy. But we do not teach heresy—we speak the truth according to the pure word of God. The very person who has come into our being is God Himself. But when He comes into us, He does not come as the Father but as the Son. The Father is the source, and the Son is the expression of the source. The expression and the source are one.

THE FIRSTBORN SON AND THE MANY SONS

Because God comes into our being as the Son, we have been born of God in the Son and have the sonship. This means that we all have become sons of God. We are not simply saved sinners but also sons born of God. This is not a small thing. Before Jesus Christ resurrected from the dead, God had only one Son, the One whom the Bible calls the Only Begotten Son (John 3:16). Before His resurrection, Christ was the unique Son of God. But after His resurrection, He was no longer the unique Only Begotten Son of God, for in resurrection He became the Firstborn among many brothers (Rom. 8:29).

How many sons does God have? On the one hand, John 3:16 speaks of the Only Begotten Son. But Hebrews 2:10 says that God is leading many sons into glory, and Romans 8:29 says that Christ is the Firstborn among many brothers. Does God have two kinds of sons? No, He has just one kind. In China, the Fukienese like to have many sons. If they cannot beget enough sons, they may buy some others. A certain man may beget only two sons and later buy another ten sons, giving him a total of twelve. These twelve sons, however, are of two kinds, the born sons and the purchased sons. Deep in his heart, this man feels that only two of his sons are sons in life, sons in reality, while the other ten are merely sons in term. Does God have two kinds of sons, the Only Begotten Son being one kind and the many sons being the other kind? No, the Bible reveals that the Only Begotten Son of God has become the Firstborn among many sons, proving that God has just one kind of son. The Firstborn is the Son of God, and the many sons are also sons of God. The Firstborn Son and the many sons are all of the same one Father (Heb. 2:11).

THE NEED FOR CHRIST TO SPREAD INTO OUR MIND, EMOTION, AND WILL

In saying that God has only one kind of son, are we saying that we, the many sons, are exactly the same as Jesus Christ? If God has only one kind of son and if we also are the sons of God, then are we not the same as Jesus Christ? How can we answer this question? Are you exactly the same as Jesus Christ, the Son of God? Jesus Christ has come into our spirit (2 Tim. 4:22; 1 Cor. 6:17). According to our spirit, we are exactly the same as Christ. But, as a human being, we also have a soul composed of the mind, the emotion, and the will. Although in our spirit we are the same as the Son of God, in our mind, emotion, and will we are not yet the same as He.

The Son of God is in us, not partially but wholly. The complete Person of the Son of God is in us. He did not cut Himself into pieces and then put a small piece of Himself into us. Christ, the Son of God, has come into us as a whole, perfect Person. Although the whole Person of Christ is in our spirit, time after time our thinking does not originate with Christ in our spirit but with our ugly mind. Perhaps even today you were thinking about a certain brother, saying to yourself, "I don't like Brother So-and-So. He should be excluded and cut off." But as long as he is a brother, whether he is good or bad, you should not say that you do not like him. This thought comes from your ugly mind, not from Christ in your spirit.

What about your emotion? When you love, do you love from the spirit where the Son of God is, or do you love from your emotion? I do not ask what you love, but from where you love—from your natural emotion or from the indwelling Christ. If we, like Christ, are sons of God, then why is our emotion different from His? Because Christ is only in our spirit. He has not yet spread into our emotion, and thus our emotion is still independent of Him.

Let us say a word about our will. Whether your will is wild or tame, it is still your will. When you go shopping, you must examine the source of your going shopping. Is the source the indwelling Christ in your spirit, or your own natural will? Sisters, when you decide to go shopping, how often do you decide from Christ and how often from your will? Out of ten times, perhaps hardly once have you decided to go shopping from the indwelling Christ. This shows that your going shopping is not pure. It is a mixture, coming mostly out of your own will. What about the decisions you make day after day? How many times do you make a decision by Christ and not by your own will? As a son of God, what is the source of your decisions—Christ or your own will? I am not talking about being good or bad, nor about anything religious. I am asking whether you make decisions from your spirit, the place where the Son of God is, or from your own will. Although we are sons of God, we must admit that most of our decisions are made from our will, not from the Son of God, Jesus Christ, in our spirit. When we sing hymns in the meetings we take one way, but when we make decisions in our practical living we take another way, the way of using a source other than Christ. Therefore, although we have Christ in our spirit, we cannot express God, because Christ is confined within us. After coming into us, He has been imprisoned within us, for He does not have the freedom to spread out from our spirit.

THE MEANING OF THE LAW OF LIFE

This again brings us to the law of life. In the previous message we pointed out that the law of life is just Christ Himself. The Christ who indwells our spirit is our life. What then is the law of life? It is life functioning. A law is an unchanging, automatic regulation. Whenever you throw an object into the air, the object will fall to the ground. This is the law of gravity which is an unchanging, automatic law.

Every life has its own law. I have often used the illustration of a peach tree. If you have a peach tree in your back yard, there is no need for you to worry that it might bring forth watermelons, or to say, "I love the form and beauty of peaches. I don't want this tree to bring forth melons. Since I'm concerned that the fruit of this tree might not have the form of a peach, I'll make some peach molds, put them on the branches of the tree, and command the tree to fit into this pattern and not to change its form." To do this would be ridiculous. But this is exactly what Christianity does. The ministers and teachers in Christianity make molds, put them on people, and charge them to live in a certain way. This is foolish. If you did this to a peach tree and the peach tree could talk, it would say, “Take your molds away from me. I don’t need any outward regulations. I have a living regulation by which I grow and bring forth fruit in the shape of peaches. The life will form the shape of the fruit.” This is a law. Every year the peach tree produces fruit with a peach shape. The same is true of an apple tree. The apple life has the apple law. As an apple tree grows, it spontaneously produces fruit in the shape of apples. This is the result of the regulation of the law in the life of an apple tree. This matter, however, is missed by Christianity.

NO NEED FOR TEACHINGS

Both in Jeremiah 31:33 and 34 and in Hebrews 8:10 and 11 we are told that we do not need anyone to teach us. If you would attempt to teach a peach tree to bring forth peaches, the tree would say, “No one is as stupid as you are. You can’t teach me. Besides, I don’t need your teaching.” Since coming to this country, especially during the first two years I was here, I told people wherever I went that they did not need to be taught. I said, “You don’t need teaching because you have life in you, and life needs no teaching.” Tell me, who taught you to breathe? Did you attend a breathing school and graduate from it? No mother teaches her children to breathe, for breathing is a matter of life. In like manner, no one instructs an apple tree to bring forth apples, because producing apples is the function of the life of an apple tree. When the apple tree functions, apples are produced. During my first two years in this country, I was burdened to tell people wherever I went that they should drop their teachings and let life work. Without one exception, I was rejected in every place. Many came to me with their Bibles, saying, “Brother Lee, in your message you said that we don’t need any teaching. Isn’t the word teaching found in the Scriptures?” I did not care to argue with them. I simply said, “If you like teaching, you may have it. But I don’t like teaching—I like life. Praise the Lord that I have life and that life is growing within me. If you like the teaching, go to the dead letters." In some places I even boldly told people, "You are as dead as a door nail. The teachings have killed you. Because you are filled to the brim with teachings, you are dead."

THE ONE LAW BECOMING MANY LAWS

We have seen that Christ is in us. This Christ equals life, and this life has its law of life. Thus, within us, we have Christ, the life, and the law. The very Christ who indwells our spirit is life, and this life has a law. In Jeremiah 31:33 the Lord says, "I will put my law in their inward parts and write it in their hearts." But Hebrews 8:10, which is a quotation of Jeremiah 31:33, says, "I will impart my laws into their mind, and on their hearts I will inscribe them." Notice that the law in Jeremiah 31:33 becomes the laws in Hebrews 8:10. Furthermore, in 8:10 the word mind is used instead of inward parts, indicating that the mind is one of the inward parts. The inward parts include at least the mind, the emotion, and the will. What is the reason for these changes? Jeremiah 31:33 and Hebrews 8:10 say that God imparts His law, or laws, into either our inward parts or our minds, and that He inscribes His law, or laws, upon our heart. The heart is composed of the mind, the emotion, the will, and the conscience. Hebrews 8:10 does not say that God imparts His laws into our hearts and inscribes them on our mind. No, it says that God imparts His laws into our mind and inscribes them on our hearts. This means that Christ has firstly come into our spirit. This Christ is the law which must spread into our mind. The spreading of the indwelling law into our mind is the imparting of this law into our inward parts. This law must also spread into our emotion and will. By spreading into our inward parts, the one law becomes many laws. Whenever we give this law the opportunity, it will spread within us. This spreading is the imparting, and the imparting is the inscribing. Thus, the Lord imparts His law into our inward parts and inscribes it on our hearts. As the Lord continues to spread, impart, and inscribe, Christ's image will be expressed in our soul, and we shall be conformed to the image of God's Firstborn Son.

THE WAY TO BE TRANSFORMED AND CONFORMED TO THE IMAGE OF THE FIRSTBORN SON

Now we know what answer to give whenever we are asked if we are the same as the Son of God. We should say, "The very Son of God is in my spirit. But my mind, emotion, and will have not yet been conformed to the Son of God. Although my mind, emotion, and will have not yet been conformed to His image, I thank God that I'm under the process of conformation. As the unique law spreads into my mind, my mind is being transformed and conformed to His image. After He spreads into my mind, my mind will be exactly the same as His. Also, He will spread into my emotion and will, making my emotion and will the same as His. Eventually, my whole being will be exactly the same as His. In this way, I shall be the image of God."

Once we have received this vision, we shall hate the religious teachings. Do not teach me to do this and not to do that. I do not care for such teachings. I only know that Jesus Christ as the Firstborn Son of God is in my spirit waiting for the opportunity to spread Himself into my mind, emotion, and will. I simply want to open to Him again and again without trying to do anything. I just open myself and say, "Lord Jesus, spread Yourself into my mind, emotion, and will. Lord, cause the unique law to become the many laws in all my inward parts. I want You to spread in me until You possess every part of my being. I don't want to love, hate, or do anything. I only want You to spread Yourself into me." In this way, we shall be transformed and conformed to the image of the Firstborn Son of God. This is God's doing, the work which He is performing in us today. This is absolutely different from religion, for it is the work of life. This life is Christ Himself with the law working in us, regulating us, ruling us, and spreading Himself into every part of our inward being.

How much we need to see this vision and empty ourselves of every religious concept. I want to drop the teachings and only love the living Christ who is in me as my life and as the unique law spreading Himself into my being. I do not care for loving or hating, for being good or bad. I do not care for anything religious. I only care for the living Christ in my spirit. Praise Him that He is in our spirit! Now He is waiting for the opportunity to get into our mind, emotion, and will that He might saturate our being with His element, causing Himself to become the very element of our being. In this way, He makes us the same as He is. We may even say that He is making Himself us. This is the working of the law of life. This is God's economy, the basic concept of the divine revelation in the Bible. May the Lord have mercy on us that we may see this vision.

THE WAY TO HAVE CHRIST SPREAD IN US

How can this Christ spread within us? Only by our eating of Him as the hidden manna. The hidden manna which we eat will become the budding element in us. As this element buds out of our innermost being, it will bud into and through our mind. This is the working of the law of life to transform us and conform us to Christ's image that we all might become His living expression.

LIFE-STUDY OF HEBREWS

MESSAGE SIXTY-FIVE

BEING CONFORMED TO THE IMAGE OF THE FIRSTBORN SON BY THE WORKING OF THE LAW OF LIFE

THE FIRSTBORN SON BEING THE PROTOTYPE

The central thought of the whole Bible is that God wants to have many sons for His expression. In order to accomplish this, God must firstly have a model, a prototype. This prototype is Jesus Christ, the Son of God. When Christ came the first time, He came as the Only Begotten Son of God. As the Only Begotten Son of God, He became a genuine man in the flesh. Although He was a real man with the human nature, He was still the Only Begotten Son of God. When He was on earth, He often called Himself either the Son of God or the Son of Man (John 10:36; 5:25; 1:51; Matt. 8:20). When the demons met the Lord Jesus, they addressed Him as the Son of God (Matt. 8:29), but He commanded them not to say this. The Lord seemed to be saying, "You demons, the followers of the Devil, must realize that I am here as the Son of Man. I have come as a man in the flesh to deal with the Devil and with you." It was by His death in the flesh that Christ destroyed the Devil (Heb. 2:14). Therefore, the Devil and all the demons were afraid of Him as the Son of Man. When the Devil tempted the Lord in the wilderness, he said, "If thou be the Son of God, command that these stones be made bread" (Matt. 4:3). The Lord Jesus replied, "It is written, Man shall not live by bread alone, but by every word that proceedeth out of the mouth of God" (Matt. 4:4). The Lord seemed to be saying, "Satan, you must know that I am here not as the Son of God, but as the very man promised in the book of Genesis. I have come as a man to bruise your head."

In today's Christianity there are the so-called modernists. In ancient times there were the ancient modernists, called the Sadducees, who believed neither in angels, nor in demons, nor in resurrection (Acts 23:8). Today's modernists are followers of those Sadducees. The Sadducees, along with the Pharisees, thought of the Lord Jesus simply as a Jew whose parents were Mary and Joseph. When Jesus came to such a person, He always stressed that He was the Son of God (John 5:17-18, 25). While the demons are afraid of Jesus being the Son of Man, the modernists, under the inspiration of the Devil, do not confess that He is the Son of God. Once the demons admit that Jesus is the Son of Man they are destroyed, and once a man confesses that Jesus is the Son of God he is saved (John 20:31). Who is Jesus? He is the Son of God and the Son of Man. To us, He is the Son of God, and to the enemy, He is the Son of Man.

Recently, two young men, aged eighteen and twenty-one, came to me with an argumentative spirit, saying, "John 3:16 says that Jesus is the Only Begotten Son of God, and Hebrews 13:8 says that Jesus Christ is the same yesterday, today, and forever. How can you say that the Only Begotten became the Firstborn? This means that Jesus has changed. But the Bible says that He is the same yesterday, today, and forever." Before His incarnation, Christ was only the Son of God; He was not a man. Was not His incarnation a great change? According to the Greek, John 1:14 says, "The Word became flesh." This certainly indicates a change. If Christ had never had such a change, we would still be in a pitiful situation. If He had not become a man but had forever remained only as the Son of God with divinity, how could we have been saved? Christ has changed. He changed from being just the Son of God into a man. Consider the Lord's incarnation. Before His incarnation, He was the Son of God, and He did not have the human nature. He was solely, singly, and absolutely the divine Son of God, having only divinity. He had no flesh and blood. But by His incarnation He changed radically. In making this radical change, He did not put off His divinity. No, keeping His divinity, He took on humanity. Hence, in His incarnation, He had divinity plus humanity. Many Christians today have only been taught that Jesus is the Only Begotten Son of God. They have never learned that this Only Begotten Son has become the Firstborn Son.

John 1:14 says that the Word became flesh, and 1 Corinthians 15:45 says that the last Adam became the life-giving Spirit. Here in 1 Corinthians 15:45 we have another "became." Firstly, Christ was the Son of God. In His incarnation He became flesh, and then, as a man in the flesh, He became the life-giving Spirit. We believe John 1:14 which says that the Word became flesh, and we believe 1 Corinthians 15:45 which says that the last Adam became the life-giving Spirit. I have been condemned as a heretic for saying that Jesus became the Spirit. According to their old, traditional teaching of the Trinity, the opposers say that the Father is the Father, the Son is the Son, and the Spirit is the Spirit. But now they are troubled, for 1 Corinthians 15:45 says that Christ became the life-giving Spirit. How many Spirits are there? There is only one. Is Christ the Son or the Spirit? He is both the Son and the Spirit and also the man. This does not mean that when Christ became the man He was no longer the Son of God, nor that when He became the Spirit He was no longer the man and the Son of God. He is all-inclusive.

Suppose you have a glass of pure water. When you add tea into it, you do not eliminate the water, do you? When you add milk, you still have the water and the tea. The water, the tea, and the milk make an all-inclusive drink. When we drink the water, we drink the tea and the milk. Basically, this drink is plain water, but it has been enriched with the elements of tea and milk. Who is Jesus today? He is the life-giving Spirit who includes divinity and humanity. Our Savior today is not the same as He was before the incarnation, nor the same as He was when He was on earth. Before His incarnation, He was purely divine, having no human element. When He was born of Mary in the manger at Bethlehem, He was mingled with humanity and put on human nature. While He was on earth, He was both divine and human. Being the Son of God and the Son of Man, He was both God and man. By His resurrection, He became the life-giving Spirit. This absolutely does not mean that He is no longer the Son of God nor the Son of Man; it means that as the Son of God He has brought the Son of Man into the Spirit.

When I was young, I was only taught that the man Jesus Christ was the Son of God. I was never told that through resurrection this wonderful God-man became the life-giving Spirit. I was only told that He died on the cross for our sins, resurrected from the dead, and ascended into heaven where He is now sitting as the Savior who is living, mighty, and able to save us to the uttermost (Heb. 7:25). But, being a thoughtful young man, I wondered how Jesus could save me to the uttermost. I said to myself, "How can this be? He is sitting on the throne in heaven far away from me, and I am here on earth far away from Him. How can He save me to the uttermost?" Although I tried to solve this problem, I could not do it. Undoubtedly, Jesus is now sitting on the throne in heaven. How then can He save us to the uttermost? He can do it because He is not only in heaven but also in our spirit. This wonderful One is in heaven and in our spirit at the same time. I have often used the illustration of electricity. The electricity which we use in our homes is also in the power plant. The same one electricity is in both places at the same time.

Christ is the life-giving Spirit. Within this life-giving Spirit there is the powerful, indestructible divinity, and there is also the proper, uplifted humanity. No humanity is as right and proper as the humanity of Jesus. Both this wonderful divinity and this uplifted humanity are now in the Spirit, just like both the tea and the milk are in the water. When we drink the water, we get the tea and the milk, and when we call on the name of the Lord Jesus, who is the life-giving Spirit, we get His divinity and humanity.

God's way is firstly to have a prototype, a model. This prototype is God the Son who came to be a man. This man, the embodiment of God, lived on earth for thirty-three and a half years, tasting and passing through all the sufferings of human life. Then He went to the cross and died. Through His death, the old creation was terminated, the problem of sin was solved, and all the enemies and adversaries of God were destroyed. His death on the cross was an all-inclusive death accomplishing everything for God's economy. But this was not the end, for He was resurrected with His divinity and humanity. His divinity was expressed, manifested in full, in His resurrection, and His humanity was transformed from a physical form into a spiritual form. This is very mysterious, and no human words can explain it. After His resurrection, He became such a wonderful One. I cannot adequately explain all the aspects of this wonderful Person. In this wonderful Person, who today is our Savior, we have the eternal, powerful, unlimited divinity; the uplifted, transformed humanity; the proper human living; the all-inclusive death that solved the problem of sin, defeated the enemy, and terminated the old creation; and the resurrection. How much we have in Him! He now expresses God in the proper humanity. Sin is under His feet, Satan has been defeated, and the old creation has been terminated. This is the prototype, the model of the expression of God.

THE IMPOSSIBILITY OF IMITATING CHRIST

Can you imitate such a One? We cannot even make imitation tea. We should not try to produce an imitation tea, but simply drink real tea. Every imitation is a falsehood. In Christianity, people are taught to imitate Christ, but it is impossible to imitate Him. We are all familiar with artificial flowers. As plastic imitations of real flowers, they have the same color, shape, and appearance as genuine flowers. When they first came out, I liked them. But after awhile I came to hate them because they have no life. Man can imitate, but he cannot create. Praise the Lord that while we cannot imitate Christ, He has a way of reproducing Himself in us.

THE SPREADING OF THE PROTOTYPE INTO OUR BEING

In a factory, a company firstly manufactures a prototype. Then the mass production is according to that prototype. In a good sense, our wonderful Christ is a prototype. God's way is to put this prototype into us. This living model is a living Person including divinity, humanity, human living, crucifixion, and resurrection. Such a model, consisting of all these marvelous elements, has come into our being. The human, religious way is to correct or improve us from without. God's way is to put Christ into us. Who is Christ? He is the Son of God, the Son of Man, and the life-giving Spirit. God has put this wonderful Person into the very center of our being. If we agree and cooperate with this wonderful One, opening up to Him, He will spread outward into our soul from our spirit. This is not imitation; it is the spreading of the prototype within our being. This is what the Bible calls sonship. Christ has come into us as the Son to be the life of the Son in us. According to Romans 8:15, we have the spirit of sonship. We have the sonship which makes us real sons. This sonship is actually the wonderful model Himself, the Firstborn Son of God. We have the life of the Son, the Spirit of the Son, and the sonship within us.

Consider once again the illustration of a tea bag placed in a glass of water. The more we stir the water, the more it will be saturated with the tea. The tea will spread into and mingle with the water until it becomes tea-water. No one can imitate Jesus. If we could imitate Jesus, then a monkey could imitate a boy. Christ is such a wonderful Person. How can we imitate Him? It is not a matter of imitating Jesus; it is a matter of being saturated with the sonship, just as water is saturated with tea. The Son, as the very sonship, has come into us. As the sonship, He is the life, the Spirit, the position, and the right of the Son. This sonship is now waiting for our cooperation that He might spread throughout our being.

THE ONLY BEGOTTEN SON BECOMING THE FIRSTBORN SON

In both Hebrews and Romans the matter of sonship is covered. In Hebrews we are told that, after His first coming, Christ eventually became, through resurrection, the Firstborn Son (1:5-6). Before His incarnation He was the Only Begotten Son of God, but through resurrection He was born the Firstborn Son of God. When I read the Scriptures years ago, I was bothered by Psalm 2:7, which says, "Thou art my Son; this day have I begotten thee." This verse is quoted both in Acts 13:33 and in Hebrews 1:5. Being troubled by this, I asked myself, "Wasn't Christ the Son of God already? Since He already was the Son of God, why did He need to be born of God in order to be the Son of God?" Later I realized that before His incarnation, Christ was the Son of God without human nature. When He was incarnated, He put on humanity. His divine element was the Son of God, but His human element was not. Hence, He had to be resurrected that His human element might be born of God. Through this birth, the Only Begotten Son of God became God's Firstborn Son. In other words, the Only Begotten Son did not have the humanity which had been begotten of God. When He became the Firstborn Son of God, His humanity was born of God. In this way He became the Firstborn Son of God, and this Firstborn Son became the prototype, the model. This is what it means to say that Christ is the Firstborn among many brothers (Rom. 8:29). The Firstborn Son is the prototype, and the many brothers are the mass production. This model today is a living Person, the Lord Jesus Christ, who is the totality of the divine sonship. When this living Person comes into us, we have the sonship and become a son of God. Now we are the sons of God, and the Lord Jesus as the model is working and moving in us.

A MATTER OF INWARD SATURATION

Although we have become sons of God by having the sonship in us, we still do not look like the Son of God. Suppose I put a tea bag in a five-gallon jar of water. The tea may be in the center of the jar, but the water does not yet have the appearance of tea. The tea must spread into and saturate the water. Gradually, all the water will be teaified and become tea. In like manner, we have been born of God by having Christ come into our spirit. But after coming into us, He has not had much opportunity to spread Himself into our being. This is not a matter of outward behavior; it is a matter of inward saturation.

Hebrews tells us that the Only Begotten Son has become the Firstborn. This Firstborn Son has regenerated many sons and now He is the model in perfection, completion, and glorification. Although He is perfect and complete, we, the many sons with the sonship within us, have not yet been perfected, completed, and glorified in this sonship. Presently, we are in the process of perfection, completion, transformation, and glorification.

SONSHIP AND CONFORMATION

The book of Romans, especially chapter eight, speaks of the same thing. Many Christian leaders have written a great deal on Romans 8. However, they mainly emphasize the Spirit. They have more or less neglected the law of life and the conformation to the image of the Firstborn Son of God. It is difficult to find a Christian book which deals with the subject of conformation. Nevertheless, conformation is necessary for the completion of the sonship, for the completion of the many brothers of the Firstborn. Although we are brothers of God's Firstborn Son, we do not resemble Him very much. We may not look much like Him today, but we are in the process of being conformed to His image. How much the sonship is completed in us depends on how willing we are to be conformed to the image of Christ. This is not a question of outward doing, but of whether or not we are willing to be conformed to the image of the Firstborn.

SONSHIP AND THE WITNESS OF THE SPIRIT

If we would know how to be conformed to Christ's image, we must read Romans 8 again and again. This chapter is a treasure chest in a treasure store. All the riches are here. In this chapter we have the law of life, the sonship, and the conformation. Verses 14 through 16 speak clearly about sonship. Verse 14 says, "For as many as are led by the Spirit of God, these are sons of God" (Recovery Version), and verse 15 says that we have received "a spirit of sonship." We know that we have received a spirit of sonship because the "Spirit Himself witnesses with our spirit that we are the children of God" (v. 16). Deep within, we have a strong witness, a strong testimony, that we are the children of God. Many of us can confidently say, "I know that I do not look like Christ, but I have the full assurance that I am a son of God. I don't care how much you criticize or belittle me, I have no doubt that I have been born of God."

We have this witness in our spirit, not in our mind. If you turn to your mind, you will begin to doubt, saying to yourself, "Probably I have not been born again. If I have been regenerated, why am I still the same? I need to say, 'O Lord, be merciful to me. If I have not been born again, cause me to be born again right now.' " In the past, I did this very thing. But while we are doubting in our mind, we have the witness deep in our spirit that we have been born of God. This is not a teaching; it is our experience. Whoever has called on the name of the Lord Jesus has been regenerated, and the spirit of sonship, that is, Christ Himself, is in his spirit witnessing to the fact that he is one of God's children. However bad we may be or however defeated we are in our Christian life, we still have the witness in our spirit that we are sons of God. This is a fact, and no one can argue with it. It is not a small thing to be born again.

THE WAY TO BE CONFORMED TO THE IMAGE OF THE FIRSTBORN

However, we should not stop with the mere fact of being born again. Romans 8 mentions the Spirit of life in verse 2, sonship in verses 14 through 16, and conformation in verse 29. We are now in the process of being conformed to the image of God's Firstborn Son. How can we be conformed? The way is found in Romans 8:6—by setting our mind on our spirit. The mind set on the spirit is life. In whatever we do and say, we must be sure that our mind is on our spirit. When our mind is off our spirit, we are like an electrical appliance which has been disconnected. If we sense that our mind is not on our spirit, we should stop and call on the name of the Lord Jesus. Many of us can testify that after simply calling on the name of the Lord Jesus, we had the sense deep within that, once again, our mind was on our spirit. Although this is a simple matter, it is very serious.

I would ask the sisters to consider their experience in shopping. Many times when you went shopping in a department store, you sensed that your mind was not on your spirit, but you still bought something. If you look back on that experience, you will realize that your mind was altogether off your spirit. If in going shopping you sense that your mind is on the spirit, you may go ahead. But if you sense that it is not on the spirit, you should stop. This is exactly what it means to walk, to have our being, according to the spirit.

WALKING BY THE INNER SENSE OF LIFE

Today the Spirit is not far away in the heavens; He is within our very being. Romans 8:6 implies that the Spirit in our spirit can be sensed. How do we know that setting our mind on the flesh is death? We know it by the inner sense. Deep within, we sense that we have been cut off and that we are dead. Whenever we have our mind set on the flesh, we have this sense within. We do not need anyone to tell us this; we can sense it ourselves. A married brother may say to his wife, "While I'm arguing with you, I'm in the spirit. Can't you realize this?" While he is saying this with his mouth, deep within he can sense that his mind is not on his spirit. I understand this quite well because I have experienced so much of it myself. Although we may tell others that we are right, in our spirit we know that we are wrong, for the sense of life does not stand with us, nor does it justify what we are doing. According to our deep inner sense, we know that we have been cut off. This is a red light in our spiritual driving. Whenever we see a red light, we must stop. When we have the sense that the inner light is green, we may then proceed. This is what it means to follow the Spirit within and to live, walk, and have our being according to the inner sense of life.

The way to be conformed to the image of Christ is by keeping our mind on our spirit. The mind of a fallen person is the representative of his whole being, for such a person does everything according to his mind. It is the same with the believers who do not walk in spirit. Thus, when our mind is on our spirit, it means that our whole being is on our spirit. In our daily living, in all that we are and do, we must have the assurance that our mind is on the spirit. To have our mind, our whole being, on the spirit is life. This is according to the working of the law of life.

LIFE-STUDY OF HEBREWS

MESSAGE SIXTY-SIX

LIVING ACCORDING TO THE LAW OF LIFE AND MOVING ACCORDING TO THE ANOINTING

The Bible reveals that God's eternal intention is to have many sons and to make all these sons the same as He is. Since God is divine and we are human, how can we become God's divine sons, becoming the same as He is in both life and nature? In order to have many sons, God in the Son firstly took the step of incarnation. By incarnation, He put on human nature. Before His incarnation He had only divinity, not humanity. But by being incarnated, He put on human nature and became a man. Although He became a man, He was still the very God, for He did not put off His divinity to become a mere human being. He was the God-man having both divinity and humanity. How wonderful that our God, the unique God, the Creator, became a man with flesh and blood! As far as human nature is concerned, He became exactly the same as we are. He was a real man with flesh and bones. Never forget that this real man, named Jesus Christ, was also God. He was the real God and the genuine man. Before He could make us like Him, He had to become like us.

THE MYSTERY OF THE RESURRECTED AND INDWELLING CHRIST

Having become a man in the flesh with human nature, Christ was crucified on the cross, was buried, and was resurrected. In resurrection He then took another step: as the last Adam, He became the life-giving Spirit (1 Cor. 15:45). This is mysterious. On the day of His resurrection, the Lord appeared to His disciples. "When the doors were shut where the disciples were for fear of the Jews, Jesus came and stood in the midst and said to them, Peace be to you." (John 20:19, Recovery Version). The doors had been tightly closed, but, to the surprise of the disciples, Jesus came. When the disciples were terrified, supposing that they had seen a spirit, the Lord Jesus said, "Behold my hands and my feet, that it is I myself: handle me, and see; for a spirit hath not flesh and bones, as ye see me have" (Luke 24:39). Speaking to Thomas eight days later, the Lord said, "Bring your finger here and see My hands, and bring your hand and put it into My side," and Thomas said, "My Lord and my God!" (John 20:27-28, Recovery Version). The Lord seemed to be saying to the disciples, "Don't think that I am a spirit. I am standing here with a body of flesh and bones. Look, the marks of My crucifixion are still upon Me. You can even touch the prints in My hands and feet."

The Lord was not only the Spirit; He was the wonderful One with a body of flesh and bones in which could be seen the prints of the nails. The wonderful Christ today is the life-giving Spirit; yet He has a body of flesh and bones. Furthermore, the New Testament reveals that this wonderful Christ is in us (Col. 1:27; 2 Cor. 13:5); He is in our spirit (2 Tim. 4:22; 1 Cor. 6:17). Christ in resurrection still possesses a body of flesh and bones and He is in us. We cannot explain how He, having flesh and bones, can be in us. This is beyond our knowledge. Although we cannot understand Him, He is real and wonderful.

According to the New Testament, Christ has had two "becomings." John 1:14 says, "The Word became flesh," and 1 Corinthians 15:45 says, "The last Adam became a life-giving Spirit." Through these two becomings, Christ has become a wonderful Person. He is the very God, the very man, and the life-giving Spirit. As the Son of God, He became a man, and after becoming a man, He became the life-giving Spirit consisting of divinity and humanity. In Him we see the real God and the genuine man. Today this God-man is also the life-giving Spirit. If He were not the Spirit, He could never have come into that locked room to meet with the disciples. Nevertheless, He still has a body of flesh and bones. I cannot explain this because I am limited, but I do know that He lives in me, and I cannot deny that He has done many things for me. Even now, He is living in and for me.

THE TWO NATURES OF THE INDWELLING CHRIST

After Christ became the same as we are in His incarnation, bringing divinity into humanity, by becoming the life-giving Spirit He brought humanity into divinity. Through incarnation and resurrection, He mingled divinity and humanity, humanity and divinity, into one. This is our Lord Jesus Christ. Not many Christians have this concept of the Lord Jesus. But this is the very Savior whom we received into our being when we believed in Him and called on His name. The Christ who dwells in us is such a wonderful One. Now He is not only the Savior and the Lord; He is also the wonderful life-giving Spirit with two natures. Most Christians have missed the mark, having never heard that the very Christ who dwells in us has the two natures of divinity and humanity, and that both these natures are in the life-giving Spirit. As the wonderful life-giving Spirit, He is now working all that He is into our being, transforming our being into His.

RELIGION MISSING THE MARK

In its concern with miracles, teachings, and behavior, Christianity misses this mark. In Christianity, there are two main religions: the religion of teachings and the religion of miracles. Many Christians are obsessed with miracles. The basic revelation of the New Testament, however, is focused on one crucial point: that Christ is one with the Father; that He sends the Spirit, who is just Himself, that He might abide in us and that we might abide in Him; and that Christ is living, moving, and working in our spirit, even transforming our very being that we might be His expression.

Although this matter is found again and again in the New Testament, not many Christians pay attention to it.

Fundamental Christianity stresses teaching, but at least two verses in the Bible, Hebrews 8:11 and 1 John 2:27, say that we do not need anyone to teach us. Hebrews 8 reveals that because we have the law of life within us, we do not need anyone to teach us. Not even the smallest among us needs anyone to teach him. First John 2:27 says that because the anointing abides in us, we do not need anyone to teach us. Since we have the law of life and the anointing working and moving within us, we do not need the outward teachings of man. Some may oppose this point, but where do they put Hebrews 8:10 and 11 and 1 John 2:27? We should take the clear and pure Word of the Bible.

In so-called Pentecostal Christianity, people stress the exercise of the gifts, especially speaking in tongues. If they come to a meeting where there is no tongue speaking or manifestation of the so-called gifts, they are unhappy. But only a very small percentage of the verses in the New Testament is devoted to speaking in tongues. A far greater percentage of the verses speak of the indwelling Christ. Here we see the subtlety of Satan. On the one hand, fundamental Christianity stresses the teachings; on the other hand, Pentecostal Christianity stresses tongues. Even when the tongues are false, they still enjoy them, and even if their prophecies are not fulfilled, they are still addicted to them. More than twelve years ago, some people prophesied that Los Angeles would fall into the ocean. Although that prophecy was not fulfilled, so many of the Pentecostalists are still addicted to their prophecies. I am not against these things, but I do have a burden for the children of God.

THE WONDERFUL NATURE OF CHRIST

When Christ came into us to be our life, He brought His nature, the nature of His wonderful being, into us. Before we were regenerated, we had only the base, corrupted nature of fallen humanity. But when we were regenerated, the highest nature was added into our being. Now there is in us the very nature of the Person of Christ. As an illustration of this wonderful nature, let us take the example of a baby. When something sweet is put into a baby's mouth, he will spontaneously swallow it. But when something bitter is put into his mouth, he will spit it out. Who teaches the baby to do this? No one. As long as the little baby is living, he does not need anyone to teach him about what is sweet and what is bitter. The baby's reaction to sweet and bitter substances is not a matter of knowledge; it is a matter of the taste of nature. A baby has a human nature, and human nature does not like the taste of anything bitter. Our nature knows what it likes and dislikes. In like manner, however babyish we may be in spiritual things, as long as we are in Christ, we have a special life nature. By coming into us, Christ brought into our being a wonderful life nature. This is not merely the divine nature; it is the divine nature with the uplifted human nature.

THE FUNCTION OF THE LIFE NATURE BEING THE WORKING OF THE LAW OF LIFE

The function of this life nature, or the nature of life, is the working of the law of life. Every life has a law. The law of a certain life is the innate ability of that life. This ability is inborn, spontaneous, automatic, constant, and instant. It always works. As long as you are a living person, this innate ability of the human life is in you. If a baby dies, it no longer has any response to sweet or bitter-tasting substances. But a living baby has the taste of nature which comes from the innate ability of life. When Jesus Christ our Lord came into us, He brought His wonderful nature into our being. The work and function of this nature are the working of the law of life. This nature functions automatically. Its function does not depend on teaching; it depends on life.

Before we were saved, we all did things which were not good, things such as gambling, drinking, smoking, dancing, and going to movies. But from the very moment we were saved, we have had something within us which troubles us and disagrees with our doing certain things. You may still go dancing, but within you is a taste which does not feel good about it. Before you were saved, the taste always felt good, but not now. We all have had this kind of experience. If you have not had this experience, I doubt whether you have been saved. This experience is the function of the life nature, which is Christ Himself wrought into our being. This function is simply the working of the law of life. There is no need for anyone to teach you. In fact, because you have Christ's nature working in you, you do not even need Him to speak to you. For example, because a mother has given her nature to her baby and because this nature works in the baby, he does not need to be taught how to react to a bitter-tasting substance. The baby's human nature functions automatically. This function is the working of the law of human life. Likewise, the function of Christ's life nature in our being is the working of the law of the divine life. It is not a matter of teaching or miracles.

CHRIST COMING INTO US TO BE A PERSON

When Christ came into us, He not only brought His nature, but also Himself as a Person. Nothing troubles us more than a person. I do not like to live alone. I like to have at least two or three others living with me. But it is troublesome to have another person living with you. When Christ came into us, He came in to be a Person. Do you realize that Christ is in you as a Person, as the living One who "bothers" you all the time? His bothering, of course, is the best bothering, for it is very profitable. Nevertheless, it is still a bothering. Before you were saved, you were free to do what you wanted. For example, you were free to go dancing. But after you were saved, especially after coming into the church life, you began to be troubled by the living Person of Christ. Daily, He bothers us from within.

THE MOVING OF THE PERSON OF CHRIST BEING THE ANOINTING

The Bible gives the moving of this Person a special term—the anointing (1 John 2:27). This term, the anointing is difficult to understand. The anointing which abides in us is the moving of a Person, the Person of Christ. This anointing teaches us. We all have something within us called the anointing teaching us in our very being. Thus, within us we have both the nature of Christ and the Person of Christ.

The anointing is the moving of the ointment within us. In typology, the ointment is composed of olive oil and some of the finest spices (Exo. 30:22-25). The main element in this composition is the oil, into which are added a number of ingredients. When the tabernacle, the utensils in the tabernacle, and the priests were anointed, all the components of the ointment were upon that thing or person which was being anointed. In typology, this ointment is Christ. The very Christ who is now indwelling our spirit is the ointment composed of the Spirit of God and other elements. As this ointment, He is moving and living in us day by day. This inward moving of the ointment affords us a living teaching. Christ teaches us in this way.

THE NORMAL LIVING OF THE WONDERFUL ONE

When Christ came into us, He brought His wonderful nature into our being. The function of this nature is the working of the law of life. Christ is also in us as the ointment which constantly anoints us. This anointing gives us a comfortable, soothing sense. Whenever the Lord Jesus teaches us from within, His teaching is that of His anointing which gives us this comfortable, soothing sense. As Christians, we all have the automatic, spontaneous, constant, and instant working of the law of life, the law which works according to Christ's wonderful nature, and we have the anointing which moves in us according to Christ's Person.

Let us use the illustration of shopping once again. Going shopping is like going to hell. After not going shopping for more than two years, I recently had to shop for a lamp. In the store I saw some very fancy lamps, but my wonderful nature did not like them. Those lamps were bitter to my taste. Some of the other lamps were like garlic to my inner taste, and my inner sense could not tolerate them. When the sisters are in a department store, many times their inner taste forbids them to purchase a particular item. This taste comes from the wonderful nature within them. Fifty years ago, I might have been able to purchase a fancy lamp. But if I did this today, I would be unable to sleep at night because of the function of the nature of life. We all have this nature with its automatic function. If you try to suppress this function, it will spring up all the more, for the more it is suppressed, the higher it rises. We all have experienced this working of the law of life.

As we have seen, we not only have this nature within us, but also a Person. Whether I should go shopping today does not depend upon the working of the nature; it depends upon the teaching of the anointing. A living Person is constantly living and moving within us. This living and moving is His teaching. If we are about to go shopping, we should open ourselves to the Lord, saying, "Lord, I'm one with You, and I know that You are one with me. Lord, do You want to go shopping this morning?" When we do this, we shall sense the anointing within. This is the moving of the living One within us. As this lovable One works in us, we sense the comforting and the soothing. How pleasant this is! Whether or not we go shopping is secondary. The primary thing is that as we look to Him and fellowship with Him, we enjoy His anointing. Whenever we are under His anointing, we know what to do. If we take a step which He does not want to take, the anointing will stop, and the soothing, comforting sense will diminish. By this we know that we should not do that particular thing. At such a time we should say, "Lord, I'm one with You. If You don't want to go, I won't go either." If we do this, the anointing and its comforting sense will return.

The living and moving of the anointing is Christ's inward teaching. We have a living Person in us teaching us all the time. Sometimes in our fellowship with the saints we may sense that the inner anointing has stopped. When we have this sense, we should stop talking. You might have spoken half a sentence, but, sensing that the anointing has ceased, you should not speak the remainder of that sentence. Simply be one with the inner anointing. Many times, however, we disregard the anointing and do whatever we want. When I was young, I told the Lord a number of times, "Lord, please forgive me and let me do this just one more time." Later I said to Him, "Lord, let me do it just once more." Many of the young people have done the same thing. Some sisters might have said, "Lord, I know that You don't want me to go shopping, but let me go this one time." Whenever you do this, you kill yourself, and it may be several days before you are living again.

What we are talking about here is neither a matter of teaching nor of miracles. It is the normal living of this wonderful One. I live absolutely according to the law of life, and I move, act, and behave according to the anointing. I do not need anyone to teach me. The wonderful nature of the life of Christ and the very anointing of the Person of Christ are more than adequate for us to live a normal Christian life. Here we have fellowship and here we grow in life. Here we have the spreading of the indwelling Christ into every part of our being and we undergo the process of God's transformation. Here we also have the church life and the real building up. And here we prepare ourselves for the Lord's coming back.

LIFE-STUDY OF HEBREWS

MESSAGE SIXTY-SEVEN

THE COMPLETION OF SONSHIP

The focus of God's revelation in the New Testament is sonship. Sonship is God's desire. God can only satisfy His desire for sonship by having His Son become the model and prototype. This prototype must be wrought into our being. What is being wrought into us is not only the Savior or the divine life, but also the prototype of the sonship, the Firstborn Son of God. As we have pointed out, there is a great difference between the Only Begotten Son of God and the Firstborn Son of God. With the Only Begotten Son, there was no humanity. He was divine, but He was not human. With the Firstborn Son, on the contrary, there are both divinity and humanity because He is not only the Son of God but also the Son of Man. The Son of Man has been brought into sonship through His resurrection. Now this Firstborn Son, constituted with both divinity and humanity, has been wrought into our very being.

PREDESTINATED UNTO SONSHIP

Ephesians 1:5 says that we have been predestinated unto sonship. Sonship is our destiny. Our destiny is not to be saved. Salvation is a process; it is not the goal but the way to reach the goal. God's goal is sonship. God's forgiveness, justification, salvation, and regeneration are all focused on sonship. God has forgiven us, justified us, saved us, and regenerated us that we might be His sons.

THE PROCESS OF SANCTIFICATION, TRANSFORMATION, AND CONFORMATION

Sonship has both a beginning and a completion. It begins

with regeneration and it will be completed with glorification. Between regeneration and glorification there is the process of sanctification, transformation, and conformation. Many Christians have heard about sanctification. However, the concept of sanctification in Christianity is much different from that found in the Bible. The vocabulary, the terminology, is the same, but the understanding is vastly different, because the dictionary of today's Christianity differs from the dictionary of the Bible. According to the pure word of the Bible, the meaning of sanctification is to be saturated with the element of the prototype. The more we are saturated by the element of the Firstborn Son as the prototype, the more we are separated unto God from the world. Through sanctification we are separated from the world, not by teachings or miracles, but by being permeated with the element of the divine and human nature of the prototype.

Our whole being is like a black spot. One day, the wonderful element of the prototype came into our spirit and sanctified it. What about the remainder of our being? We must admit that it is still very dark. Although you may consider yourself to be good, moral, ethical, and even "spiritual," you are still dark. Perhaps you are in a dark grave. Whether you are good or bad, right or wrong, moral or immoral, ethical or unethical, "spiritual" or unspiritual, your being is still dark. Whenever others contact you, they sense your opaqueness. You dwell in the gloomy dungeon of your religion and ethics, and there is nothing transparent about you. Because you are so dark and non-transparent, you need to be sanctified by having the wonderful element of the prototype saturate your being. The more Christ spreads into you, the more you will be sanctified and separated from the world. This is sanctification.

Transformation is related to sanctification. The more we are saturated with the element of Christ, the more we are sanctified, and the more we are sanctified, the more we are transformed. As we have pointed out several times, transformation is not an outward change, adjustment, or correction. It is an inward metabolic change, a change in life, nature, and form. Sanctification is for transformation and transformation is for conformation. We must be transformed in order to be conformed to the image of the Firstborn Son of God (Rom. 8:29). By the Lord's mercy, we are in the proper church life being sanctified, transformed, and conformed to the image of God's Firstborn Son. This is deeper, higher, and more profound than being moral, ethical, or even "spiritual." Some teachings regarding so-called spirituality are merely vanity. Genuine spirituality is conformation. Being spiritual depends upon being conformed to the image of the Firstborn Son of God. No human effort, labor, or imitation can manufacture this. It can only be produced by the indwelling prototype, the real and living Firstborn Son of God, who automatically works in us. As He works in us by the law of life, He continually anoints us from within.

THE LAW AND THE PROPHETS

Because we are sons of God according to the law of life and the anointing, we are God's people. God is our God according to the law of life and the anointing. In ancient times, God called His people, the children of Israel, out from among the Gentiles and gave them the law. God was their God and they were His people according to the outward law of letters. If they were right with the law, then they were right with God. Since the people went astray from the law, the prophets came in. Hence, the Old Testament is composed of the law and the prophets.

The law corresponds to God's unchanging nature. For time and eternity, God's nature will remain the same. Although the law does not change, the prophets do change. A prophet of God may tell you one thing today and the opposite thing tomorrow. If you consult a prophet about going to a certain place today, he may say that it is all right to go, but if you ask him the same question tomorrow, he may tell you not to go. God is living. As the living God, He is the highest Person, having the full right to tell us one thing today and another thing tomorrow. Due to this, the word of the prophet may change. The law is according to God's nature, but the prophets are according to God's activity, God's move. God may want you to stay where you are today, but tomorrow He may want you to go elsewhere. The law is always the same for everyone. For example, the law commands you to honor your parents. God will never tell you to honor your parents today and then command you to hate them tomorrow. No, the law remains constant. However, if you read the Old Testament, you will see that the prophets differ from one another. In ancient times, God was a God to His people according to the law and the prophets, and God's people were a people to Him also according to the law and the prophets.

What do we have in the New Testament which corresponds to the law and the prophets in the Old Testament? For the law, we have the law of life, and for the prophets, we have the anointing. Today, God is our God according to the inner law of life and according to the anointing, and we are His people according to the inner law of life and according to the anointing. The inner law of life corresponds to God's nature, and the anointing corresponds to God's move. The law of life always remains the same. As far as the law of life is concerned, there is no change either with you or with others. If you attempt to go to a movie tonight, the inner law will forbid you. It will also forbid you tomorrow and at any other time. The anointing, however, may change. Tonight the anointing may not allow you to go to the department store, but tomorrow the anointing may encourage you to go. While the law of life will never allow you to buy a fancy lamp, the anointing may or may not allow you to go to the department store. Furthermore, the anointing may permit one brother to go shopping, but it may forbid another brother to do the same thing. By this we see that the anointing changes. If I intend to speak to you in a condemning way, the law of life will always say, "No, don't do that." But whether or not I should speak on Hebrews in the meeting tonight depends on the anointing. Tonight the anointing may encourage me to speak on Hebrews for forty-five minutes, but in the next meeting the anointing may say, "Don't speak anything in this meeting. Be at rest." By all these examples we see that the law remains the same but the anointing constantly changes. It is according to this law and this anointing that we are a people to God and God is a God to us. How different this is from religion! Here there are no outward regulations, forms, rituals, or controls. There is only the law of life and the anointing.

Approximately fourteen years ago, I was invited to the home of a Jewish brother in New York. His background was that of a typical orthodox Jew. He told me that the orthodox Jews do everything according to a verse in the Old Testament. When they go to bed at night, they must even place their shoes in a certain direction according to a verse in the Old Testament. They are very "scriptural" and religious. There are many regulations among them, but no life. These orthodox Jews think that they are the people of God and that God is their God according to their religion. Actually, God is far away from them. He is not their God and they are not His people according to their way. But today God is our God according to the law of life and the anointing.

THE LAW OF LIFE AND THE ANOINTING VERSUS REGULATIONS AND ORGANIZATION

Although we may be clear about these matters doctrinally, we may not be clear about them experientially. In the church life we should live according to the law of life and move according to the anointing, but we have gradually come to live according to regulations and move according to organization. In the beginning, the church life was not like this. It was living, and we lived according to the inner law of life and moved according to the anointing. Gradually, however, our living according to the law of life developed into a habit, and the habit became a regulation. Thus, today we live according to regulations and move according to organization. Because we have become organized, we neglect the anointing. How I long to see the dear ones coming to clean the meeting hall according to the anointing, not according to any arrangement or organization. If in the service groups we care for who is first, second, and last, we shall have an organization. In an organization there is no need to pray, to contact the Lord, and to move according to the anointing, because everything is arranged, and we are told what to do and when to do it. A brother who is not a leading one may say, "I am neither the first nor the last. Whatever I do will be all right. I don't need to look to the Lord about what time to clean, because the time has already been announced. If I am a few minutes late, it will not make any difference." When this brother arrives, he will stand around waiting to be told what to do. If the leading one does not come, he will not know how to function. This is not the service we see in the New Testament.

THE LIVING REVEALED IN THE NEW TESTAMENT

According to the New Testament, the law of life is written into our being. In fact, even the writer Himself is in us. By coming into us, He brings both His nature and His Person into us. The nature works and the Person moves. Hence, we must live according to His nature and move according to His Person. We must clean the meeting hall according to His moving. Do not care about your rank in the church service. Only care for the living Person within you. This is the living found in the New Testament. Compared with the Old Testament, the New Testament is quite short. The Old Testament may have over a thousand pages, but the New Testament has less than three hundred pages. Christianity has become a religion of teachings and miracles. I hope that in the Lord's recovery we shall realize that we do not need the teachings and miracles found in religion. We simply need to live according to Christ's wonderful nature and move according to His wonderful Person. Do not depend upon regulations, arrangements, or organization. Move and act according to the living Person within you. If we do this, we shall enjoy God and become His people, and God will become so living, rich, and enjoyable to us. He will be our God, not according to regulations, but according to the inner law of life and the anointing. This is the working of the divine and human nature of the wonderful One.

THE NEED TO BE RESCUED FROM RELIGION

You may wonder why I am against religion. It is because I have passed through so many things, especially the teachings and speaking in tongues. In the past, I taught many people how to speak in tongues. But after a period of time, I saw that speaking in tongues only stirred people temporarily and that the result was not much of life. I was also in fundamental Christianity where I learned the teachings of the Bible. More than forty-five years ago, I became familiar with all the types, teachings, and prophecies. These teachings made me dormant for seven and a half years. Due to this, I have the sure standing to declare that we do not need the teachings in letters. After a certain time, I became involved with the Pentecostal movement. Now I have been commissioned and burdened by the Lord to minister Christ as life to His people. Only when you have been wholly rescued from the other things will my burden be discharged. The Spirit knows how much you need to be delivered. Not only those in Christianity but even the church people need to know the sonship. We must see that life is the only way the sonship can be brought to completion within us. The working of the law of life within us is for the carrying out of the sonship.

GOD'S WAY OF LEADING THE MANY SONS INTO GLORY

Hebrews 2:10 says that God is leading many sons into glory. How will God bring the many sons into glory? Will all the Christians remain the same day after day until they are suddenly transported into glory? No indeed! In 1 Corinthians 15 Paul says that the resurrection is like the growth of a plant. After a seed is sown into the earth, it dies and begins to grow. At first, the plant is a tender sprout. This tender sprout must grow until it reaches maturity and blossoms. The blossom is its glorification. The plant, unlike a mushroom, is not glorified suddenly. No, it is glorified by its gradual growth. Likewise, we all have been regenerated and are growing. Many are like tender sprouts which have a long way to go before they can be glorified. The distance between regeneration and glorification encompasses the process of sanctification, transformation, and conformation to the image of the Firstborn Son of God. A few among us who have grown in life throughout the years are on the verge of glorification. They are ready to blossom. How about you? If you are still a tender sprout, then you are not ready to blossom. You must continue to grow until you reach maturity. Then, at the time of your maturity, you will blossom into glorification. In this way God will lead the many sons into glory.

GLORIFICATION—THE COMPLETION OF SONSHIP

At this point, we need to read Romans 8:29 and 30: "Because whom He foreknew, He also predestinated to be conformed to the image of His Son, that He should be the Firstborn among many brothers; and whom He predestinated, these He also called; and whom He called, these He also justified; and whom He justified, these He also glorified" (Recovery Version). Verse 30 does not say, "And whom He justified, these He brings to heaven." No, it says, "These He also glorified." We must also read Romans 8:16 and 17: "The Spirit Himself witnesses with our spirit that we are the children of God. And if children, heirs also; heirs of God and joint-heirs of Christ, if indeed we suffer with Him that we may also be glorified with Him." Verse 17 does not say that we may be brought to heaven. No, it says that we "may be glorified with Him." The goal is glorification. This glorification is the perfection, the completion, of conformation. In other words, glorification is the perfection and completion of sonship. The sonship has begun in us, but it has not been perfected and completed. Presently we are undergoing the process of sanctification, transformation, and conformation. Daily we are being saturated by the indwelling wonderful One. He is constantly seeking an opportunity to spread Himself into every part of our being. He desires to saturate us until we are sanctified, transformed, and conformed to His image and reach the perfection and completion of sonship. This is God's desire today.

This is not a matter of being right or wrong, proud or humble, ethical or unethical. It is not even a matter of being "spiritual" or unspiritual. God does not care for these things. Thirty years ago, I was with some people who sought spirituality. But the more we pursued it, the more it eluded us. Even the pursuit of "spirituality" is vanity. God's intention is to conform us to His Son. His Son, the prototype, has been wrought into us and is awaiting the opportunity to saturate us with His element. We must cooperate with Him by living according to His nature and moving according to His Person. We should say, "Lord, I don't care for spirituality. I only want to live according to Your nature and move according to Your Person." By the Lord's mercy, I have been living and moving this way throughout the years. All I have received for it is condemnation. I have been condemned because I refuse to tolerate the religious things. Having passed through the teachings and the Pentecostal things, I can testify that they neither work nor supply us. Although they may help to a small extent, they do not supply us. But if you live according to the nature of this wonderful One and move according to His Person, you will be abundantly supplied and others will be supplied through you. This is what the church life needs today.

The church life in the Lord's recovery is absolutely and wholly different from Christianity. Because we are different, we are condemned as being heretical. I admit that we are different, but I do not admit that we are heretical. Our understanding of the Bible is according to the pure Word with the light from the heavens. We do not care for traditional teachings. We only follow the pure Word of God in the

Bible. Although we are absolutely different from tradition, we are absolutely according to the Bible.

The working of the law of life and the moving of the anointing will complete the sonship in us. We all have been destined to sonship and we are presently undergoing the process of becoming the full sons of God. Today our law is the law of life and our prophet is the anointing. As we have seen, this law is according to Christ's nature and this prophet is according to His Person. We live according to His nature and move according to His Person. This is our standing. I look to the Lord that we all might see this. This must be ministered to all the saints in the church life. We do not care for the teachings in letters; neither do we care for the outward miracles. We only care for the inward law of life and the inward anointing.

Our God is real and living. He is real and living within us, not according to religion, nor according to our human thought. Having passed in the Son through incarnation and resurrection and having both divinity and humanity, He has come into us as a living Person with a wonderful nature. His nature is now functioning within us. We have seen that the function of His nature is the working of the law of life and that the moving of His Person is the anointing. In the church life we are not concerned with doctrine, teaching, miracles, and "gifts." We are daily dealing with a living Person and His wonderful nature. His nature constantly remains the same, working within us to spread His element into our being. And His anointing continually guides us in our actions, movements, and behavior. It is by His nature and His Person that we live and move. In this way He gradually works Himself into our being. The more He is wrought into us, the more we become the sons of God in perfection and glorification. If we see this, we shall not be distracted by other things. Christianity is a religion, but the church is a matter of life. This life is simply the wonderful One, the One who has passed through incarnation and resurrection and who is now the life-giving Spirit consisting of divinity and humanity. As we live according to His nature and move according to His anointing, we shall grow and be saturated, transformed, and conformed to His image until we are ripened in the sonship and prepared for the rapture. Then we shall be ready to meet Him.

LIFE-STUDY OF HEBREWS

MESSAGE SIXTY-EIGHT

LIVING ACCORDING TO THE NATURE OF GOD

The focus of the divine revelation in the Bible is sonship. God's intention is to express Himself. In order to have His expression, He must have many sons. Do not think that salvation is the center of God's revelation. The center of His revelation is sonship. God wants many sons. When God sent His Only Begotten Son into the world, His intention was to beget many sons through Him, making Him His Firstborn Son. Although the Lord Jesus came the first time as the Only Begotten Son of God, when He comes the second time, He will come as the Firstborn Son (Heb. 1:6). Being the Firstborn Son means that He is the first among many sons, the Firstborn Son among many brothers (Rom. 8:29).

THE SIGNIFICANCE OF SONSHIP

In the Bible, the significance of sonship is the expression of the Father. A son always expresses his father. When we look at a boy, we see in him the expression of his father. A human father may need only one son to express him, but the divine Father, who is marvelously and wonderfully great, needs millions of sons to be His expression. One day the earth will be filled with the sons of God, and wherever we go, we shall see the image of the Father, the expression of God. If you read the New Testament carefully, you will see that God does not want a company of sinners who have been redeemed, cleansed, and brought into heaven. This is meaningless. God wants many sons to be His corporate, universal expression. Wherever these sons are, there the Father will be expressed. This is sonship. "Behold, what manner of love the Father hath bestowed upon us, that we should be called the sons of God" (1 John 3:1). This is the basic concept in the Scriptures.

THE SONS OF GOD HAVING THE DIVINE NATURE

If you spend time with a father and his son, you will discover that the son not only bears his father's image, but that he also carries his father's nature. As his father's son, he has his father's nature. Likewise, if we have truly been born of God, then we must have His nature. The nature in life is a very significant thing. Every life has a nature. The nature of a life is the very substance of that life. If there is no nature, then there is no life. Regardless of the kind of life it is—vegetable, animal, human, or divine—as long as it is a life, it has a nature. The substance and essence of a life are in its nature. What the nature is, that is what the life is also. An apple tree produces apples because it has an apple-tree nature. In like manner, a dog has a dog's life because it has a dog's nature, and a man has a human life because he has a human nature. Could we be human without having a human nature? Of course not. We are human beings because we have a human nature. Because we have a human nature, whatever we do, think, and say is human. Similarly, whatever a dog does is according to the dog's nature. This nature is the source of the law of life.

THE LAW OF LIFE BEING THE WORKING OF THE NATURE OF LIFE

The law of life is not only according to the nature of life; it is also of the nature of life. The law of life comes out of the nature of life. Because a particular life has a certain nature, it has a certain law. An apple tree has an apple-tree nature; hence, its law is the law of the apple-tree nature. Why does an apple tree bring forth apples? Because the life law regulates it according to its life nature. In this we see that the law of life is actually the working of the nature of life. When the nature of a life works, the law of that life also works. Suppose we have two trees, an apple tree and a peach tree. If these trees fail to bring forth fruit, we cannot see the law of life. But if the apple tree spontaneously produces apples and if the peach tree spontaneously produces peaches, we see the working of the law of life regulating each tree according to the nature of its life. Therefore, the law of life is simply the working, the functioning, of the nature of life.

Suppose a dog and a man are standing in front of you. If the dog and the man do not move, you will not see the function of the law of life. But if the man behaves in a human way and if the dog begins to bark, these actions will indicate the working of the nature of each life, which is the law of that life. You may command the dog, saying, "Little dog, you must imitate this man. I charge you to follow him and to be one with him, saying and doing whatever he does." But the more you speak this way to the dog, the more it will react according to the working of the law of its nature. If, on the contrary, you command the man to behave like the dog, he will find it impossible, for he does not have a dog's nature.

THE ONLY BEGOTTEN SON BECOMING THE PROTOTYPE

We have seen that God's intention is to have many sons. His way to have the many sons is to make His Only Begotten Son the prototype. Christianity misses this, having never seen the difference between the Only Begotten and the Firstborn Son of God. Most Christians consider the Only Begotten and the Firstborn Son as being the same. However, there is a great difference between Jesus' being the Only Begotten Son and His being the Firstborn Son. As the Only Begotten Son, He was not the prototype. In order to be the prototype, He had to become the Firstborn Son of God. In the Only Begotten Son there was only divinity, no humanity, but in the Firstborn Son of God there is humanity as well as divinity. This humanity has been "sonized," that is, it has been begotten of God in Christ's resurrection. In Psalm 2:7, God said to the Son, "Thou art my Son; this day have I begotten thee." Because Christ's human nature, His humanity, has been "sonized" in His resurrection, He is no longer merely the Only Begotten Son of God, but the Firstborn Son of God with divinity and humanity. Hence, He is the prototype.

THE MASS PRODUCTION OF THE PROTOTYPE

God's way to mass-produce this prototype differs from the mass production in a factory. In a factory, a company first produces a prototype and then mass-produces the models according to the prototype. God's way is to work His living prototype, the Firstborn Son, into our being to be our life and nature. This life is the divine life, and this nature is the divine nature. Now God is working to spread this divine life and nature into every part of our being, transforming our natural being into that of the Firstborn Son of God.

According to Romans 12:2 and 2 Corinthians 3:18, this is transformation. In the process of transformation, the living prototype spreads from our spirit into every part of our being. Transformation wholly depends upon the imparting of the law of life into our spirit. The law which has been imparted into our spirit is the function of the divine life; it comes from the nature of the divine life. Since the day this law came into our spirit, it has been awaiting the opportunity to spread into our mind, emotion, and will. Eventually, it will spread throughout our being. As it spreads, the one law will become several laws. Because the law is the working of the nature of the divine life, when it works, it produces sonship. Its working will always produce the image of God.

THE DIFFERENCE BETWEEN THE LAW OF LIFE AND THE ANOINTING

With scarcely one exception, nearly all Christians have been distracted from this law and have gone astray from it. Out of a hundred Christians, probably less than five know this law or have heard about it. In Christianity, there is no word or message on the law of life. Because most Christians have gone astray from the law of life, there is the need of the anointing.

What is the difference between the law of life and the anointing? As we have seen, in the Old Testament there were the law and the prophets. The Old Testament comprises these two categories of the divine word. In ancient times, the Old Testament was even called "the Law and the Prophets." What is the difference between the law and the prophets? Why did God, after giving the law to Moses, still need to use Elijah, Isaiah, Jeremiah, Ezekiel, Daniel, and the other prophets? We have pointed out that the law was given to be a testimony of God, having been given according to the nature of the Lawgiver. Since the laws you make express the kind of person you are, your laws are your testimony. The law was the testimony of God because it testified what kind of God He is. It testified that He is a holy, righteous God, a God of light and love. Since He is such a God, His law had such a nature. In nature, the law was righteous, holy, and full of light and love. Hence, the law was God's testimony. God chose Israel from among the nations to be His people, desiring that they would be His people according to what He is. Because the law revealed what God is, the children of Israel had to be God's people according to His law.

In the first chapter of Isaiah we see that the children of Israel went away from God and His law (Isa. 1:4, 10). If the Israelites had not gone astray from God's law, there would have been no need for the prophets. But because the people did go astray, God sent the prophets to call them back by rebuking, charging, and directing them to return to God's testimony. God did not intend to make the ministry of the prophets the standard. The standard of His testimony was the law, and the ministry of the prophets was to bring the off-center people back to the center, to bring God's straying people back to God's testimony. Hence, the ministry of the prophets was to recover God's fallen people to His law.

We have seen that the Old Testament comprises the law and the prophets. With what is the New Testament composed? It is composed of the law of life and the anointing. The law of life replaces the law of letters, and the anointing replaces the prophets. In a previous message we pointed out that the law was given to testify of God's nature and that the prophets were sent to represent God's Person. Therefore, the prophets spoke, saying, "Thus saith the Lord." In the law we have the nature of God, and in the prophets we have the Person of God.

THE PRESENCE OF GOD AND THE NATURE OF GOD

Which do you prefer to have—the nature of God or the presence of God which represents His Person? Every Christian regards the presence of God as dear and precious. In Christianity there is much talk about the presence of God. We are told that the presence of God should mean everything to us and that we must do all things in God's presence. In Christianity, the believers are taught to live and walk in God's presence, and a number of books have been written about living in the presence of God. But where can you find a book telling you to live according to the nature of God? If we have the revelation, we shall prefer the nature of God to the presence of God. I may live in a certain brother's presence, loving him and walking with him. Nevertheless, he remains a Caucasian and I remain a Chinese who lives in the presence of a Caucasian. What does this mean? Nothing. Simply to live and walk in the presence of God without having His nature in you means very little. For thousands of years, the angels have been walking in the presence of God, but they have never satisfied Him. Only one thing can touch God's heart—to have a people who live and walk according to His nature. For a flea to walk in your presence means nothing, but for a flea to live according to your human nature means a great deal. Thus, walking in the presence of God means little, but living in and by His nature has great significance. However, most Christians only know the presence of God; they do not know His nature.

THE NEED TO BE DELIVERED FROM WORK TO LIFE

Because most Christians know only the presence of God but not His nature, it is easy for them to grasp the matter of the anointing. However, it is difficult for them to get into God's nature. Recently, many have testified that formerly they served in the church by organization, but that now they serve by the anointing. For example, some have said that now they come to clean the hall by the anointing. This is wonderful. However, after having been sent by the anointing to clean the meeting hall, with what life do you clean? Perhaps you clean in your old life. While the anointing is for moving, the law of life is for living. Few Christians pay attention to life. When they hear about the things of life, they respond like the Jews in ancient times, saying, "This is a hard word; who can hear it?" (John 6:60, Recovery Version). But whenever a revivalist comes to stir people up, they are excited. Anointing is for activity, but the law of life is for being.

God does not care for what we do; He cares for what we are. The record of Jacob in the book of Genesis illustrates this. Throughout his entire life, Jacob did nothing. Although he performed no outstanding work, he was constantly under the process of God's transformation. Even when he was in his mother's womb, God used Esau to deal with him. As we have pointed out in some of the life-study messages on Genesis, his family functioned as a team to transform him. After Jacob had fled his home and had come to the home of his Uncle Laban, Laban's hand was upon him. Do you think that Jacob's life was a waste? Should someone have gone to Laban's home and spoken to Jacob, saying, "Jacob, why are you here wasting your life? Why don't you go to the mission field or establish a church? Why don't you have a Bible study in your home? You are wasting your time living here under Laban's hand." But those years were not a waste. God does not want your work. He can do anything He wants simply by speaking. He calls things not being as being (Rom. 4:17). If He wants something, He simply needs to say the word and it will come into being. He does not need you to help Him. But God cannot just say, "Jacob, you must be Israel." In order for Jacob to become Israel requires a long process. This is life.

We all must be delivered from work to life. Actually, it matters little whether you stay home or go to clean the meeting hall. I am not saying that the hall should not be cleaned. I am saying that whether we stay home, come to the meeting hall, or even enter into heaven means nothing. What counts is what we are. If you stay home, you should stay there not only according to the anointing, but also according to the law of life. Some brothers may be guided by the anointing to stay home, but while at home they fight with their wives because they do not live according to the law of life. When they are home, their wives may pray, "Lord, have mercy on me and rescue me. Send my husband to the hall. I don't want him to stay home because he bothers me so much." When such a brother is at home, he bothers his wife; and when he comes to clean the meeting hall, he bothers the brothers. Wherever he goes, he troubles someone because he has no change in life. Consider a dog. A dog will bother people wherever it goes. Do not think that if a dog is in an unclean place, it will bother someone, but if it is in your living room, it will not bother anyone. The environment may change, but the dog remains the same. Likewise, whether I stay home or come to clean the meeting hall, I am still what I am. My wife may be afraid of my being home, and the brothers may be afraid of my coming to the hall, saying, "Be careful with this brother. Don't touch him. He is very fragile. If you touch him, he will break." This brother may have the anointing, but he does not live according to the law of life. The law of life, not the anointing, is what changes us.

THE FUNCTION OF THE ANOINTING

Although the anointing does not change us, it has a good function. Firstly, it rebukes us, and secondly, it tells us to return to the law of life. Perhaps all of us have misunderstood 1 John 2:27, which says that "the same anointing teacheth you of all things." The anointing does not teach us to do everything; it teaches us to abide in Christ. Some brothers and sisters may wonder whether or not to go shopping and they pray to the Lord, saying, "O Lord, should I go shopping or stay home? Lord, grant me the anointing." But the Lord may say, "My anointing doesn't care for your going shopping or staying home. My anointing only cares that you abide in Me. As long as you abide in Me, you may go anywhere. If you abide in Me, whatever you do will be all right." If we abide in Christ, we may go anywhere. But remember this crucial clause—"if we abide in Christ." As long as we abide in Christ, God does not care where we go or what we do. Many who are concerned about marriage pray to the Lord regarding it, saying, "Lord, should I marry this one?" Some can testify that although they prayed in this way, the Lord never answered their prayers. Many young brothers have prayed, saying, "Lord, let me know whether this sister is the dear one You have chosen for me." But the more the brothers pray like this, the more confused they will be. I know of some sisters who have prayed for ten years about getting married without receiving an answer. If the Lord were to answer them, He would probably say, "I don't care about your marriage. I only care whether or not you abide in Me. If you abide in Me, you may get married. But if you do not abide in Me, you should not even marry the best brother." The only thing that counts is whether or not we abide in the Lord. In God's economy, it is not a matter of our doing; it is absolutely a matter of our being. It is a matter of what we are. And what we are depends upon the life according to which we live day by day.

BEING RECOVERED TO THE LAW OF LIFE

In ancient times, the people of Israel got off the center, which is God's law, and God sent the prophets to bring them back. Today most Christians are away from God's center, which is the law of life. Therefore, the epistle of 1 John was written to the degraded Christians, calling them back to the anointing. The law of life is a basic matter. Because it is basic, it is mentioned in the book of Romans, a book of basic teachings. The anointing, on the contrary, is not mentioned in any of the basic books. Rather, it is mentioned in a book dealing with degradation, because many Christians had been distracted by the teachings of the antichrists. In the First Epistle of John, John told them to care for the anointing. John seemed to be saying, "The anointing tells you what to do and where to go. Don't listen to the teachings of the antichrists—obey the anointing. The anointing will bring you back to the law of life." First John 2 brings us back to Romans 8. But if we are truly living in Romans 8, we do not need 1 John 2. Likewise, if the Israelites had never gone astray from God's law, there would have been no need for the prophets. From now on, we should live according to the law of life and not just move according to the anointing.

God cares for His nature, but His presence is our safeguard. God's nature is within us, and we must live according to it. This means that we must live according to the law of life. However, we are often distracted. In times of distraction, God's presence will watch over us, observe us, and warn us. If we stray from the law of life, the anointing will say, "No!" After we say, "Lord, I repent," then the anointing will tell us to return to the law of life. In a foregoing message, I said that we must live according to the law of life and move according to the anointing. The anointing represents God's presence directing us, correcting us, and bringing us back to His nature. We must live according to the law of life. This means that we must live and walk according to God's nature.

Why is it easy to grasp the matter of the anointing but difficult to get into the law of life? It is easy to know a brother by his presence. With even a short glimpse, we can easily recognize his presence. But it takes a great deal of time to get into his nature. Perhaps his wife, who has lived with him for many years, is the only one who has gotten into his nature. We may know this brother's face, but we do not know his nature. In like manner, it is easy to apprehend God's presence, but it is difficult to know His nature in our being. Merely to tell people to walk in the presence of God is rather natural and religious. It is not life. But to know God's nature within our being and to live according to it is exceedingly deep. This is what God desires.

GOD'S CONCERN

God is not concerned with what we do; He is concerned with what we are according to His nature within us. He does not care much about what we say to our wives, but He does care about the life by which we speak to them. According to what nature do you speak to your wife? Sometimes you may say, "Dear, I love you." This is a good word, but in saying it you might be playing politics. Any kind of political talk, even if it is about love, is like rotten honey because it originates from our corrupted nature. It does not issue from the divine nature in your being. Likewise, God does not care whether or not you go to the mission field. He cares about the life by which you go to the mission field. I do not go to any sinful place, because the divine nature in my being does not allow me to go. I do not live according to religion or regulations; I live according to the divine nature in my being. When we live day by day according to the divine nature, we shall be saturated with Christ and transformed to His image. During the twenty years he was in Laban's home, Jacob did nothing, but he underwent a good deal of transformation. Jacob was not instantly transformed; it took more than twenty years.

In the church service, it is not just a matter of serving according to the anointing and of not serving according to organization. If our service is merely like this, before long we shall be fighting with one another. We may even fight over cleaning the chairs. One brother may say, "Don't you know that this is my territory? Don't touch it and don't bother me. Go someplace else to clean." This brother's way of cleaning is according to his corrupted nature. Although he might have been sent by the anointing, he cleans according to his fallen nature. Following the anointing is not as important as living according to the law of life. We may all be sent by the anointing to clean the meeting hall, but still not have any building among us. Everyone may become independent, saying, "Don't bother me. We are in the new church service. In the old service we had an order and a sequence. According to that order, I was last and could not say anything. But now

I'm the same as everyone else. Don't tell me what to do. I'm not under you—I'm under the anointing." If this attitude does not come out immediately, it will come out after a few weeks. A brother who claims to be following the anointing but who does not live according to the law of life may say, "We are not in the organization—we are in the organism." But this is the "organism" of a corrupted nature. If we live this way, there can be no building. I cannot find a verse in the New Testament which says that the building comes from the so-called anointing. But in Romans and Ephesians we see that the building issues from the growth of life. The more we grow, the more of the building we shall see.

How can we grow in life? By obeying the anointing which teaches us to abide in Christ. To abide in Christ is to live according to His nature. His nature is working and functioning within us. As we have seen, the functioning of the nature of life is the law of life. The more we live according to this law of life, the more we become the kind of being God desires.

THE CONSUMMATION OF GOD'S WORK

According to the Bible, God's work throughout the centuries will consummate in the New Jerusalem. It will not consummate in a work, for there will be no work in the New Jerusalem. The New Jerusalem will be a being bearing God's image. Hence, the very being of the New Jerusalem will be God's expression. The church life today must be a miniature of the New Jerusalem.

We should not care much for work, but we should care for our being, for what we are according to the nature of God within us. I would like to hear a brother or sister testify, saying, "I thank God that in recent days I have been living according to the inner law of life. Last night I was distracted from the law of life, but the anointing checked me and told me to return to the divine nature within me. After a few minutes I did return, and now, once again, I am living according to the law of life." I would also like to hear a brother testify, saying, "This morning I began to speak to my wife in a nice, yet political, way, but because my speaking did not correspond with God's divine nature within me, I could not even complete one sentence." Learn to live according to the law of life. The anointing is God's presence to direct us, to correct us, and to bring us back to the law of life. It is the law of life which works in us to transform us. If the brothers and sisters in the churches live according to God's divine nature in their being, the Lord will have a prevailing testimony on earth today. This testimony will shame the enemy and bring the Lord back. This is what the Lord is waiting for. We all must see that it is not merely a matter of following the anointing; it is absolutely a matter of living according to the law of life, according to the functioning of the divine nature of God in our being. As God's nature works within us, it makes us exactly the same as He is, transforming us and conforming us to the image of the Firstborn Son of God. In this way, God will have the complete sonship for His corporate expression.

LIFE-STUDY OF HEBREWS

MESSAGE SIXTY-NINE

THE FUNCTION OF THE LAW OF LIFE

In the tabernacle we see a clear picture of the anointing and of the law of life. The anointing was upon the tabernacle, for the tabernacle and everything in it were anointed with oil (Exo. 40:9). As we have seen, the inmost item of the tabernacle was the tables of the law, the testimony of the law. By this picture we see that the anointing was outside but that the law of life was inside. In the Old Testament the anointing was for inauguration into function. For example, there was an altar in the outer court, but before it was anointed it could not function. Likewise, although the tabernacle had been erected, it could not function until it had been anointed. Hence, anointing is neither a matter of life nor of nature; it is a matter of inauguration for function. Every time you are anointed, you are inaugurated into your function.

The law was not spread upon the tabernacle; it was placed in the center of it. At the center of God's people, the children of Israel, was the tabernacle which was enclosed by a wall of linen curtains. Within the tabernacle was the Holy Place, within the Holy Place was the Holy of Holies, within the Holy of Holies was the ark, and within the ark was the heart of the universe, the place where God was. In ancient times, God did not require His people to work nor to engage in certain activities; He required them to live and walk according to the law. If anyone was wrong with the law, he was wrong with God. God was the God of the children of Israel according to the law, and they were His people according to the law.

In the New Testament the anointing is mentioned several times. For instance, in Luke 4:18 the Lord Jesus said that He was anointed to preach the gospel, and Hebrews 1:9 says that the Lord was anointed with the oil of gladness. The Apostle John also speaks of the anointing a number of times (John 9:6; 1 John 2:20, 27). The New Testament also mentions the inner law of life which comes out of the nature of God. In the New Testament the divine life is referred to more than a hundred times. This divine life has been imparted into our being. Most Christians pay attention to the outward anointing, but neglect the inner law of life. Many of those in the so-called Pentecostal movement talk about the anointing. Although they may experience the anointing which is upon the tabernacle, they do not enter into the ark in the Holy of Holies and touch the tables of the law.

Our eyes must be opened to see that the Lord's recovery is not so much in the anointing as it is in the law of life. In the New Testament the anointing is mentioned less than twenty times, while life is mentioned more than a hundred times. Many Christians are familiar with verses like Galatians 2:20, which says, "Not I, but Christ liveth in me," and Galatians 4:19, which says, "My little children, of whom I travail in birth again until Christ be formed in you." Although many Christians know these verses, they pay no attention to them. Rather, the Pentecostalists devote their attention to the manifestation of the gifts. In His recovery, the Lord turns us again and again from the outward to the inward.

THE NEED TO TOUCH CHRIST HIMSELF

Although we are saved and in the church life, many of us are still in the church's outer court. Some might not even be in the outer court, but on the street outside the outer court. Others have gone farther than the outer court, having passed from the altar and the laver into the Holy Place where they enjoy Christ as the showbread and the lampstand, as the life supply and the light of life. Thank the Lord that many of us enjoy Christ in this way. However, this is still only the Holy Place. We must come forward and enter into the Holy of Holies. In the Holy of Holies we touch the ark, Christ Himself. The hidden manna, the budding rod, and the law of life are all in Christ. How we need to touch Christ Himself! Christ today is in the Holy of Holies. The Holy of Holies signifies that our spirit has been joined to heaven, for the very Person of Christ is the ladder joining earth to heaven and bringing heaven down to earth (John 1:51). If we continually touch Christ in our spirit, we shall enjoy Him as the hidden manna and as the budding rod. Then our daily life and walk will not be according to any teaching, work, activity, or movement, but according to the law of life, the function of the nature of the Triune God. God's nature is now moving and working within us, adding Christ's element into our being, transforming us, and producing the many sons whom God desires.

THE DIVINE BIRTH

Most Christians are off-center. When I was young, I read a number of books about victory over sin. Those books presented various ways to overcome sin. However, not one of those ways ever worked. Eventually, I discovered a precious word in 1 John 3:9: "Whosoever is born of God doth not commit sin; for his seed remaineth in him: and he cannot sin, because he is born of God." Whether we sin or not depends upon whether or not we have been born of God. He who has been born of God never sins. Furthermore, 1 John 5:4 says, "Whatsoever is born of God overcometh the world." Therefore, overcoming sin and the world does not depend upon a method; it depends upon the birth of God. When we were born of God, the divine life with its nature and law was imparted into our being. As long as we have this divine life with its nature and its law, everything will be all right.

THE SHAPING FUNCTION OF THE LAW OF LIFE

In understanding the Bible, we have been influenced too much by our natural concepts. In the past, I said that the function of the law of life was to regulate us. According to this concept, if we are about to argue with our wife, the law of life will regulate us. This teaching, which is according to our natural concept, is not accurate. Consider an apple tree. Its apple-tree life has the apple-tree nature, and issuing from this apple-tree nature is the law of the apple life. Does the law of life in the apple tree regulate it from being wrong? Absolutely not. The law of the apple life does not function this way. How then does it function? As the life of an apple tree grows, its law shapes the form of its life. Thus, when an apple tree bears fruit, it bears fruit with the proper form, the form of apples. The same is true of a peach tree. Hence, the law of life does not regulate us from doing wrong; it regulates the shape of life.

If a certain life does not grow, the law of that life cannot function. The law only operates as the life grows. The law of life does not primarily function in the negative sense of telling us what not to do. No, rather, while life grows the law of life functions in the positive sense of shaping us, that is, conforming us to the image of Christ. This is the function of the law of life.

Do not think that the law of life will always correct you. For example, when you are about to exchange words with your wife, the law of life will not merely restrict you from arguing with her. The working of the law of life is not as low as we have thought. Due to our human, natural, religious concept, we have greatly depreciated the function of the law of life. We all have been sin-centered and sin-conscious, but we should be neither sin-centered nor sin-conscious. Though we are occupied with overcoming sin, the world, our ugly flesh, and our bad habits, God would say, “Forget about these things! Don’t you realize that on the day you were regenerated you were transferred out of one realm into another? Will you please forget about the old realm?” Praise God that we have been born of Him! This divine birth has transferred us into a new realm, a realm in which there is no sin, world, or flesh. In this realm there is the function of the law of life. Remember that the law of life is not mainly regulating us; it is mainly shaping us, conforming us to the image of Christ.

In the past, I saw this matter of the law of life, but being under the influence of my natural understanding, I thought that the function of the law of life was mainly to regulate us. This natural understanding frustrated the vision of the function of the law of life. Recently, I was rebuked by the Lord. The Lord asked me, "Who told you that the law of life mainly regulates? You cannot find such a word in the Bible. Why don't you use the words of Romans 8:2 and 29?" The law of life in Romans 8:2 does not regulate us from being wrong. This concept is according to our human, natural, ethical, religious understanding. We need a vision of Romans 8:29. We are now in another realm and do not need any regulations. In this realm there is no sin, world, flesh, or self. Consider two trees, an apple tree and a peach tree. They have no sin, world, flesh, or self. But both trees have a law of life which shapes them. This shaping by the law of life is the meaning of the word "conformed" in Romans 8:29. The law of the Spirit of life conforms us to the image of the Firstborn Son of God. As the life grows, the law conforms us to the image of Christ. How can Christ be formed in us? Only by the positive working of the law of life which shapes us to His form. What a difference between this reality and our natural concept!

Satan is subtle. Although the Bible tells us clearly of the function of the law of life, we have been blinded by our natural concept. Many saints who were seeking after the Lord but who were blinded by their natural concept have written books on how to overcome sin. If you do not try to overcome sin, it may lie dormant in you. But if you try to overcome it, it will say, "What! Are you trying to defeat me?" Many of us have some weak points. If we pay no attention to them, they will remain idle and dormant. But if we are aware of them and, for the sake of our holiness, try to overcome them, they will rise up and defeat us. It is best for us not to touch them. Praise the Lord that we have had a new birth, a divine birth. In this new birth there are no weak points. There is only the divine life with the divine nature and the divine law which shapes us and conforms us to the image of Christ. However, this shaping requires the growth in life, for the law of life only functions as life grows. The law of life does not regulate us from sin, because it is not in the realm of sin; it is in the realm of the divine life where there is no sin, world, flesh, or self. As life grows, its law works, not mainly to regulate or correct us, but to shape us, to conform us to the image of the Firstborn Son of God. Eventually, through the function of the law of life, we all shall become the mature sons of God, and God will have His universal, corporate expression.

A WORD OF CONCLUSION

God's intention is to produce many sons that He may have His full, corporate expression. This is the unique goal of God's divine economy. His Only Begotten Son, who is the express image of His substance and the effulgence of His glory (1:3), became a man to declare Him and to express Him in human life. In His humanity, Christ, the Only Begotten Son of God, expressed God. In His humanity, He was also begotten of God through His resurrection to be the Firstborn Son of God with both divinity and humanity. Now, as the Firstborn Son of God with divinity and humanity, Christ is the model, the pattern, for a mass production. Through His resurrection, all those who believe in Him have also been regenerated to become the many sons of God. We, the many sons of God, who are the many brothers of the Firstborn Son of God, are those who constitute the church.

The Firstborn Son of God has been perfected and glorified, and He is now the Pioneer who has entered into the realm of glory. He is also the Captain of our salvation who has fought the battle and who is taking the lead to bring us, His many brothers, into His glory. Now in the heavens as our High Priest, He is ministering into His believers whatever He is, whatever He has accomplished, and whatever He has attained. His ministry in the heavens is a better ministry, a more excellent ministry (8:6), because through it He ministers to us in His resurrection life all that He is and all that He has done. On the one hand, He is in the heavens as the High Priest ministering life into us, and, on the other hand, He, as the life-giving Spirit, is now in our spirit to be our life. In this life within us, which is the wonderful Christ Himself, there is the law of the divine life which constantly works and functions in the depths of our being.

According to the type, the law was God's testimony, for the law was the expression of what God is. This law was placed into the ark which was in the Holy of Holies of the tabernacle, God's dwelling place. The book of Hebrews tells us that we are the many brothers of God's Firstborn Son (2:11), that we are the church (2:12), that we are the partners of God's appointed and anointed One (1:9, 3:14), and that we are also the house of God (3:6). The house of God is the equivalent of God's dwelling place which was typified by the tabernacle wherein was the Holy of Holies. Therefore, we, the many brothers of God's Firstborn Son, the church, the partners of God's appointed and anointed One, and the house of God, are God's real dwelling place today. In this dwelling place there is the Holy of Holies. This Holy of Holies is our regenerated human spirit which is joined to the heavens where the glorified Firstborn Son of God is.

Christ is now both in the heavens and in our spirit. In the heavens, He, as the High Priest in His kingly and divine priesthood, is ministering into us all that He is and all that He has done. In our spirit, He is working within us as the life-giving Spirit with the law of life. Thus, His ministry in the heavens and His working in our spirit correspond with each other. His ministry in the heavens is carried out by His functioning, His working, in our spirit. Whatever He is and whatever He has done are now being wrought into us through the working of the law of life in our spirit.

By means of the clear picture portrayed by all the furniture in the tabernacle, we can see that the aim of the experience of this wonderful Christ is to bring us into the Holy of Holies so that we may fully participate in the function of the law of life. As we have seen, we firstly experience Christ as our redemption at the altar in the outer court. After this, we experience Him as the washing and cleansing Spirit at the laver. This brings us into the Holy Place where we may enjoy Christ as our showbread, the bread of life, and as our lampstand, the light of life. Following this, we experience Christ as the incense altar through which we are ushered into the Holy of Holies. Here in the Holy of Holies, we enjoy Christ as the hidden manna and as the budding rod. By this enjoyment we are enabled to participate fully in the law of life. It is only here in the Holy of Holies, that is, in our regenerated human spirit, that we can fully participate in the function of the law of life. The function of the law of life is not mainly to regulate us from doing wrong, but to conform us to the image, the form, of God's Firstborn Son that we may become the same as the model.

The book of Hebrews is very deep. It is deep in its revelation of Christ as the appointed and anointed One of God, as the Pioneer into the realm of glory, as the Captain of salvation leading His many brothers into His glory, and as the High Priest in His kingly and divine priesthood ministering all that He is in His divinity and humanity and all that He has attained into His brothers to make them the reproduction of Himself so that God may have His corporate expression. Hebrews is also deep in its unveiling of the fact that this wonderful Christ is now joined to our spirit, which is the very Holy of Holies of God's dwelling place today, to be our life with the law of life functioning and working to conform us to His image. This is the most crucial point of the whole book of Hebrews. It is the vital focus of the experience of the Christ revealed in this book. This is why 4:12 says that our human spirit must be divided from our soul so that we may enter into the Holy of Holies to touch the throne of grace and enjoy grace in our time of need. And this is also why we are charged in 10:22 to come forward with boldness to the Holy of Holies so that we may participate in the function of the law of life. It is through this functioning of the law of life that the very Christ who is now ministering in the heavens can minister all that He is and all that He has accomplished and attained into our very being, not only to transform us, but also to conform us to His image so that we, His many brothers, may be absolutely the same as He is. In this way,

God will have the many sons as His full expression. This is the goal of God's divine economy. This goal can only be attained by Christ's ministering in the heavens as the High Priest and by His working as the life-giving Spirit within our spirit through the law of life.

About the Author

Witness Lee was born in 1905 in northern China and raised in a Christian family. At age 19 he was fully captured for Christ and immediately consecrated himself to preach the gospel for the rest of his life. Early in his service, he met Watchman Nee, a renowned preacher, teacher, and writer. Witness Lee labored together with Watchman Nee under his direction. In 1934 Watchman Nee entrusted Witness Lee with the responsibility for his publication operation, called the Shanghai Gospel Bookroom.

Prior to the Communist takeover in 1949, Witness Lee was sent by Watchman Nee and his other co-workers to Taiwan to ensure that the things delivered to them by the Lord would not be lost. Watchman Nee instructed Witness Lee to continue the former's publishing operation abroad as the Taiwan Gospel Bookroom, which has been publicly recognized as the publisher of Watchman Nee's works outside China. Witness Lee's work in Taiwan manifested the Lord's abundant blessing. From a mere 350 believers, newly fled from the mainland, the churches in Taiwan grew to 20,000 in five years.

In 1962 Witness Lee felt led of the Lord to come to the United States, and he began to minister in Los Angeles. During his 35 years of service in the U.S., he ministered in weekly meetings and weekend conferences, delivering several thousand spoken messages. Much of his speaking has since been published as over 400 titles. Many of these have been translated into over fourteen languages. He gave his last public conference in February 1997 at the age of 91.

He leaves behind a prolific presentation of the truth in the Bible. His major work, *Life-study of the Bible,* comprises over 25,000 pages of commentary on every book of the Bible from the perspective of the believers' enjoyment and experience of God's divine life in Christ through the Holy Spirit. Witness Lee was the chief editor of a new translation of the New Testament into Chinese called the Recovery Version and directed the translation of the same into English. The Recovery Version also appears in a number of other languages. He provided an extensive body of footnotes, outlines, and spiritual cross references. A radio broadcast of his messages can be heard on Christian radio stations in the United States. In 1965 Witness Lee founded Living Stream Ministry, a non-profit corporation, located in Anaheim, California, which officially presents his and Watchman Nee's ministry.

Witness Lee's ministry emphasizes the experience of Christ as life and the practical oneness of the believers as the Body of Christ. Stressing the importance of attending to both these matters, he led the churches under his care to grow in Christian life and function. He was unbending in his conviction that God's goal is not narrow sectarianism but the Body of Christ. In time, believers began to meet simply as the church in their localities in response to this conviction. In recent years a number of new churches have been raised up in Russia and in many European countries.